How Hard It Really Is

A Short, Honest Book About Depression

Cover art by Rob Connelly. http://heyitsrob.com

Editor's note: This publication is an informative guide on the subject matter. It is not intended to replace or countermand the advice of your physician. If expert assistance or counseling is needed, the services of a competent professional should be sought.

Park, J.S., author.
   How hard it really is: a short, honest book about depression / J.S. Park. —First edition.
Includes bibliographical references.

ISBN 978-0692910368
   1. Depression, Mental. 2. Cognitive Therapy. 3. Depression, Mental—Religious aspects—Christianity 4. Mental health 5. Healing—Religious Aspects—Christianity

Printed in the United States of America.
10 9 8 7 6 5 4 3 2 1

Citation Information:
J.S. Park, *How Hard It Really Is* (Florida: TWE Media, July 2017) p. _

Join me in the journey of faith.

Wordpress. jsparkblog.com
Facebook. facebook.com/pastorjspark
Tumblr. jspark3000.tumblr.com
Podcast. thewayeverlasting.libsyn.com
Twitter. twitter.com/pastorjs3000
YouTube. youtube.com/user/jsparkblog

Dedicated

For my wife, J,
for life.

For my dog, Rosco,
for laughs.

Table of Contents

"At the moment what I heard was God saying,
'Put down your gun and we'll talk.'"[1]
— C.S. Lewis

---

[1] The final interview with C.S. Lewis, conducted by Sherwood Wirt on May 7, 1963. Published in *Decision* magazine, Sep. 1963

Disclaimer

I am not a licensed therapist.

This book is about the conversation around depression. It should not replace the advice of your physician.

This book is also about my experiences with depression.

I majored in Psychology for my bachelor's and I have a Master's degree in Divinity (MDiv). I was a pastor for seven years in two different churches, mostly dealing with youth and college students and their families. I've been a hospital chaplain for about two years (which requires intense accredited training). My chaplaincy work includes: attending every death, attending every Code Blue, next-of-kin notification, advising patients on end-of-life decisions, and grief and crisis counseling. Many of the patients I've visited are dealing with grief or depression or both.[2]

In January of 2004, I attempted to kill myself by ingesting half a bottle of acetaminophen. I was placed under the Baker Act, an involuntary hold by the state for those who have harmful thoughts towards themselves or others, and after two nights in a hospital, I was sent to a care facility for another two nights. I've been diagnosed with clinical depression, and my only personal experience with antidepressants is that I tried them for two days before quitting. I struggle with depression to this day.

My family has a history of depression and suicidal ideation. My late maternal grandmother suffered from dementia (and possibly Parkinson's disease), and my uncle has schizophrenia. They both

---

[2] The National Comorbidity Survey shows that 29% of adults with medical conditions also have mental illnesses.

lived in the house until my parents divorced when I was fourteen.

In the following pages, any technical information regarding depression has been carefully cited. I highly recommend further research on your own, as new studies constantly emerge and can contradict one another.[3] There's also not a single consensus in the medical community about the causes and treatments of depression; the "experts" are still learning how to navigate through it.

This book is filled with triggers. While I have tried my best not to be overly gratuitous, the subject matter necessarily entails that I do not shy from its depths.

Whenever I insert my own opinion, I start with the phrase, "I believe," "I think," "I have a theory," or similar self-referential phrases. Please feel free to disagree or to engage in dialogue with me.

There have been many good books on depression, including Andrew Solomon's magnum opus The Noonday Demon and Dr. David Martyn Lloyd-Jones' Spiritual Depression. They cover much more ground than I could, and I recommend them to you.

Any identities and identifying markers in the book are altered for privacy of the individuals.

---

[3] The field of psychology is currently struggling with a methodology problem called the Replication Crisis, in which studies are becoming less and less reliable due to the inability to replicate. However, the emerging thought is that these different outcomes are actually highlighting previously unknown variables, which is helping to widen knowledge rather than contradicting the original results.

Preface
Sneak Attack Phantom

Depression is a rumor, until it is reality, and then it's as if nothing else was ever real. Still, no one will believe you. I find it hard to believe it myself. I wrote this book for those who believe, and for those who want to.

Depression is, when you're in it, absolutely ridiculous, because it seems to be the most important thing in the world when it's happening. At the same time, it robs the world of any importance, as if nothing could ever happen again. It is a nightmare of infinity wrapped in cellophane.

The whole thing sneaks up with a dreadful, creeping stealth, "like feeling your clothing slowly turn into wood on your body."[4] It is remarkably invasive, a highly honed, weaponized virus of the mind.

Whenever I describe it happening, it sounds absurd. And it is.

At the grocery store I'm thinking about how to grill this salmon, and my chest folds inward, a curled up canvas of wax paper in a cruel, gnarled fist. It's the familiar feeling of drowning, of disappearing in frothing acid. I fight back both tears and laughter, and I tell myself, *Everything's fine, everything's fine,* a cognitive trick to pull myself out of the falling, but nothing is fine, nothing is fine. There's nothing I can do. My basket full of trinkets is weightless and a wrecking ball.

---

[4] Andrew Solomon, *The Noonday Demon,* (NY: Scribner, 1961) p. 50

I see people rushing to somewhere, but the illusion of significance slips away in a long, defeated sigh. I hate this part. My shoulders crumple because I've stopped holding them up. I can barely look at the cashier and I don't remember paying when he hands me the receipt. I can't turn on music in the car; it's unbearable to turn the wheel. I'm someone else's ghost in someone else's body.

I wish I could say it gets easier each time, but I never know how long it's going to be.

I never know when the colors will come back.

I never know if this will be the one that wins.

Clinical depression will often do whatever it wants with you. It has no rules or code or fairness or dignity.

I have every reason to be *fine*, but depression is a dirty sneak attack that leaves me completely naked and debilitated. It's a liar that sells truth: a false reality that says how-I-feel is who-I-really-am. And when a grafted lie overruns the truth, it doesn't matter that I have "every reason" to be fine: the lie has switched every goalpost and sunk the baseline.

Depression is the worst kind of lie, in that it not only attacks your self-worth and value, but steals the meaning out of words like "self-worth" and "value." It is cold inertia, slowing down worlds in orbit. It leaves you carved open, constantly bleeding out, unable to retain the vital stuff that makes life. There's spiritual discombobulation; every emotion is a phantom limb, and no amount of affirmation about "life-gets-better" can reach me there.

The thing is, when I'm hit with depression, I already know what to do. I know I have to fight for air. I know I have to crawl for every inch of territory that's stolen. I know I cannot make decisions unless I talk with someone first. I must reach for my phone. I must reach for every scrap of surface to escape this tunnel. I must remind myself that there's so much worse in the world, and that the war inside cannot compare.

I know. None of this makes the fog any easier.

By the tiniest shred of sight, I must crawl.

This book is about the crawling.

—

This book is also a primer for those who don't suffer from depression, but want to understand.

Here's what I've discovered: no matter how much someone wants to sympathize, any time I talk about depression, I see eyes glaze over.

Some will find my earlier description of depression to be difficult to read because it's so painful. Others will find it difficult to read because it's so over-the-top.

All this talk on mental illness can sound theatrical and maudlin, a "downer," embellished in hindsight, a hackneyed purple prose that induces eye-rolling.

I get it. I'm with you.

I have to admit that even as a fellow fighter of depression, I tend to evaluate "depressives" with a grain of salt and skepticism. Some cases appear to be a self-indulgent product of the *need for drama and attention,* a hyperactive imagination, a young artsy moodiness without a leash. And in some cases, all of that could be true.

Those with depression can come across as overwrought and heavy-handed. As the screenwriters say, we drop too many anvils. I am Chekhov's bazooka, exchanging subtlety for soap opera, overplaying my hand.

My humble plea is that you'd still hear me. That you'd endure a bit of cheese and flourish. That even when the "skeptical gag reflex" is set off, you could push past it towards empathy. I hope that amidst the lofty and grandiose, you may hear what is unheard.

—

Why a book on depression?

Imagine a crime scene where everyone speculates with conspiracy theories. The approach would be unreliable and the conclusion inaccurate. There would be panic, wrong solutions, and more confusion.

Depression itself is encased in misconceptions. The pain of going through mental illness is already hard enough; to add myths only makes it that much more unbearable. By investigating the mystery of depression, we can remove some of the fog around the fog. We can add layers, depth, and nuance to clear up the many misinterpretations. *It's in sharing what we* go *through that we are empowered to make it through together*. I wrote this book as a conversation so we can talk differently about depression with the thoughtfulness it deserves.

Depression can feel like a solo sport. There's no team backing you up. It's like swimming or gymnastics; once you get going, it's up to you to make it to the other end of the pool or the mat. Most of the resources I found on depression began with the "solo" premise: It's up to you, go get help, here's this method, try this and this. But that sort of individualized isolation was very vacuum-ish to me. Life doesn't work in such a frictionless shrink-wrap. We affect others in a causational web and we need their help, too.

So I try to answer some questions. *How do we collectively get through depression? How do we manage the stress and cause-and-effect and even the global consequences of depression? How do you talk to your friend about it?* I want to bring in every person involved, because depression affects families, cultures, marriages, churches, all of it.

This discussion is a game of telephone. "I'm depressed" sounds like "I'm antisocial" to most people. When I got to the research and surveys, it was even worse than I had thought. There was this nearly impermeable membrane around the discussion of depression. My whole goal is to peel back that weird membrane around depression so, if anything, there would be more empathy on every side.

There are three purposes in these pages, for both the person wrestling with depression and for those who are not:

1. To help us be free from some of the myths about depression.

2. To give us tools to fight through depression.

3. To help your friend fight through depression.

I've conducted multiple informal surveys, with over 40,000 words in responses from nearly two hundred individuals, so that a myriad of voices can be heard. You will hear from many fellow fighters of depression. You'll see you're not alone.

I'm afraid that at some point, I will let you down. I'll come up short. I'll have missed an opportunity. I'll eventually say something that will warrant a really poor review.

That's the bad news. **I don't have a magic formula, a six-step cure, or a silver bullet.** I wish I did. But I don't believe there's a right combination of words that will unlock depression.

The best thing we can offer each other is *each other,* our set of experiences, our voices, our ears, so that the tunnel is less intimidating and the light is not as distant as it was.

I wish I had more than this. I wish I could cover every angle. Maybe, though, I can cover a few.

At the very least, I can tell you what I've been through, and what's worked for me. And maybe some of that will work for you, too.

Please feel free to skip around, browse through, or go directly to the chapter you need.

Part I
The Crime Scene

Through Wet Streets and Back Alleys,
Unraveling the Myths and Mystery
of the Unseen Villain

*An investigation through the myths
of depression, and trying to find a
better way to communicate
through the mystery.*

Chapter 1
How Hard It Really Is

What It Feels Like

I've had clinical depression for as long as I can remember, a lifelong whisper on my shoulder feeding poison in my ear—but as familiar as it is, I've found it hard to show others that it's really there.

I can show you an open gash, a purple bruise, a swollen eye, and even hidden monsters like cancer or blood clots can be laid bare. Describing depression, however, is like relaying someone else's dream with someone else's tongue.

Knowing what it *feels like* might seem gratuitous, but **without an accurate description of our experiences, we're severely limited in sharing, consoling, and empathizing with our deepest wounds**. We then float in a starless space, without reference or a vantage point to heal.

I'm hoping to make the abstract into a concrete tangible.

Since an estimated 350 million people suffer from depression around the world, then the other 95% of the world is standing on the outside. There's one death by suicide every forty seconds worldwide, and over half of the 40 million Americans with a mental illness don't seek treatment for depression.[5,6]

---

[5] "WHO | Depression," *World Health Organization,* Updated Feb. 2017
http://www.who.int/mediacentre/factsheets/fs369/en/
[6] "SAVE | Suicide Facts," *Suicide Awareness Voices of Education,* Reviewed 2014

We may have already heard these numbers in statistical whirlwinds of TED Talks and blog posts. If you're like me, stats can be numbing until they're pinned down to a single image—an impoverished child, a spouse with heart disease, or a disaster-torn city. The problem here's that the popular image of depression—a sad, sour thespian—is quickly laughed off stage.

This is all the more reason we need to talk about *what it's like*. **Depression thrives on its unrelenting invisibility,** creating a fatal cycle in which its own camouflage is the very mechanism by which it destroys. It thrives by hiding. It feels silly to bring up depression, which is isolating—and to feel isolated often feeds into the isolation, which is depression's most insidious strategy.

By talking about how hard it really is, we can find refuge in our connection.

—

In an online survey, I asked, *"For fellow sufferers of de-pression, what does it feel like?"*

I wanted to know if we could converge on a common ground.

The responses were overwhelming, alarming, and heart-breaking. Some of them were:

It feels like you're constantly drowning but you just won't die.

I call it the Deep Purple Morass. Clinging molasses, seductive but disheartening.

My mind takes temporary, yet complete residence in the times I have hurt people I love. I think myself doomed to a lifetime of continuing in those patterns of hurt and shame, and am consumed with terror over what effect that will have on the relationships I treasure. I feel powerless against myself.

A two ton weight that follows you around. It constantly holds up a mirror to the past. It keeps a log of all the abandonment, pressure, loss, rage, and loneliness, and constantly tries to break the record. It always says you're not good enough.

Spiraling circles of powerlessness. You think something can change, and right when you think it will, you turn around and realize you're headed right back to where you came from.

It feels like forever while it's there and as though it never happened when it's over.

Depression feels like a tease. You want to die but you can't.

It felt like I had the floor under my feet, then the floor broke and I fell. Then I felt like I landed on another lower floor. Just when I thought I was better, I'd fall even further.

It feels like the question, *Why?*

For me, ***depression is a fog in which I collapse inward and lose all sense of myself.*** I know when it begins, like I've stepped into a sweeping cold, and I know when it ends, as if I've stepped into new air, like the cold was never there.

One of the most vivid descriptions of depression I've read is by author and journalist Tim Lott, who also digs into the physical symptoms:

"I start to stumble when I walk, or become unable to walk in a straight line. I am more clumsy and accident-prone. In depression you become, in your head, two-dimensional—like a drawing rather than a living, breathing creature. You cannot conjure your actual personality, which you can remember only vaguely ... You live in, or close to, a state of perpetual fear, although you are not sure what it is you are afraid of."[7]

These descriptions were so different, but I found that depression *could be* communicated, often with similar imagery

---

[7] Tim Lott, "What does depression feel like? Trust me – you really don't want to know," *The Guardian,* Apr. 19, 2016
http://www.theguardian.com/commentisfree/2016/apr/19/depression-awareness-mental-illness-feel-like

and running themes. It was not some amorphous shape-shifter. The singularity was blurry, but visible.

Yet over and over, each respondent felt that their depression was misunderstood, not only with a lack of empathy, but with an abrupt scorn. Many were tired of explaining themselves. When I asked respondents, *What kind of dialogue have you found helpful?*—the replies revealed that just having dialogue was a rare miracle.

In other words, *we do have plenty to say about depression, but it seems no one wants to listen, which only imprisons those with depression even further.* There's no shortage of words to describe depression, but there's a short-circuit in the delivery of the description.

The talk of depression comes with its own built-in blind spot, a chasm around the abyss.

My Broken Brain Doesn't Get Your Broken Brain

Why does this happen? Why doesn't depression get a fair hearing?

I feel like that scientist in a disaster movie who keeps yelling, "The flood/earthquake/meltdown/alien-invasion is coming!"—and everyone just shrugs.

I'm afraid that telling someone, "I have depression" tends to come off as begging, "Please believe me!" It gets written off as melodramatic and self-absorbed, usually with ridicule and resentment.

Try a thought experiment. When you read the previous descriptions of depression in the last few pages, did you feel more compassion or more contempt? Was there trust or suspicion? Engagement or detachment?

I believe the dilemma with describing depression happens because:

1) When it's expressed, it's often hand-waved as nothing more than "sadness" or "introversion" or "laziness."

2) Unless someone has experienced depression, then reaching out is usually ineffectual. It's like describing the Mojave to a polar bear.

I'll be the first to admit that I also raise an eyebrow when others tell me about their depression. While it's true that some confessions of depression might be "crying wolf" (a lot more on this in Chapter 6), *we tend to rush too quickly to the other extreme. We often don't engage confessions of depression with serious discovery.*

Part of the reason we do this is purely from reflex: by design, we like to dismiss stuff. We each have *heuristics*, these internal rules about how we see the world, and since it's a big world, we use the least amount of cognitive faculties to generalize the broadest sweep of input. In other words, we turn a single scene into a whole story. It's an instant process.

There's an *effort-reduction framework,* like a constant Occam's razor, pruning what we see into bite-sized chunks so our brains can save time and energy.[8]

We make **snap judgments** based on the information at hand, no matter how little is at hand. It's a necessary adaptation to survive. We must make quick decisions with little info around the clock. But the side effect is that *our conclusions are often found by the path of least resistance.* Part of this means we're biased towards the visual. We don't naturally empathize with an "internal storm."

This is why we cringe at an open wound, while a migraine gets, "Drink some cold water." In martial arts training, I've heard countless times: "He's not bleeding so he's fine."

I've seen this snap judgment as a common attitude in the hospital all the time. When we talk about car accidents, cancer, or the common cold, we use assured language. It helps that these injuries can be seen quickly. Yet describing depression can feel pathetic and pointless, even with a shared well of vocabulary. A patient with cancer is treated much differently than a patient with depression, *even though both diagnoses can lead to a terminal result.*

I don't mean to equate these two diagnoses, but rather to make a larger point: that a clear-cut physical problem has measurable categories, while psychological issues are bound in metaphors, images, and narratives, which are beyond our

---

[8] This "cognitive laziness," or mental shortcut, is a field of study in social psychology. Other subcategories of heuristics include the rule of thumb, stereotyping, or profiling.

conventional grids.[9] The former has visual cues that demand a crisis response. The latter defaults to a hasty, harmful prejudice. A surgeon gets the VIP seat; a psychologist gets called a fraud.

It's no wonder that depression is seen as "psychosomatic" or a "hot mess." Add to that *confirmation bias,* in which we affirm only the ideas that we want to confirm, in a culture where depression is seen as whiny and wasteful, and this conversation was never on the table.

All this to say: *When it comes to validating mental illness, the deck is stacked against us.*

Dark, Unknowable Void

Fortunately, the tide is changing. Recently, a YouTube personality loudly declared that "depression is the stupidest thing in the world," and thousands of commenters voiced their outrage.[10] I've seen a healthy, growing awareness in the public square in which we're finally approaching mental illness *prima facie,* at face value.

And yet, I wonder if "outrage" is the right response, even to someone who says depression is "the stupidest thing in the

---

[9] Fortunately, scientific advances are attempting to "see depression" by imaging technology or chemical tests, but 1) they are still in themselves only limited diagnoses using a confined range of vocabulary, 2) the "cure" is not yet aided by such technology, and 3) the resources to conduct such tests are beyond many sufferers of mental illness.

[10] ""Depression is the stupidest thing in the world." – CinCinBear," *Reddit,* May 28, 2017, https://www.reddit.com/r/LivestreamFail/comments/6dwbzn/depression_is_the_stupidest_thing_in_the_world/

world." Yes, that's indefensible, but maybe there's a deeper reason it was said.

This leads to a point which is hard for me to admit, but harder for me not to.

I have a lot of sympathy for both sides of this conversation. **There's an elusive element to depression itself, a dark void of "the unknowable"**—which means depression, in the end, is impossible to both fully understand and describe, even for the person with depression. Those who *want* to understand mental illness still struggle.

This doesn't make it okay to dismiss depression, but I can see why it happens. *Maybe depression itself has pulled off the devil's trick of convincing the world it doesn't exist.*

In the many descriptions of depression that I read, as vivid as they were, I saw a point where there was a loss of words to meet on even ground. *There was a void in the middle of the consensus.* This frustrated me to no end, and it was a bit terrifying.

Maybe it was from a limitation of language, or the lack of practice in expressing ourselves, or the unspoken wall between all human connection in that we are each "alone" in our own heads, never fully known as we are, separated by the opaque nature of our flesh.

Or depression is just that clever: *it exists in an uncanny valley of unreality where it's never fully knowable.* Eventually, there's a threshold in which depression cannot be fully articulated, no matter how much you try. It is dark matter, swirling in dead space, pushing on orbits without a trace.

Not only that, but depression can be so different from person to person that we might never comprehend all its intricacies. Mental illness is notoriously difficult to diagnose for those exact reasons.[11] If each depressed person is already different than the next, then the 95% of the world population without depression will find it that much harder to understand.

There was a similar bank of imagery from each survey, but each reply in itself was uniquely painted. It would be harmful to treat every case the same way.

As cruel as it is to dismiss depression, it's also just as crass to expect total understanding from case to case. The spectrum is so buck-shot with words like *numbness*, *lethargy*, and *vacuum* on one hand to *mania*, *irritability*, and *panic* on the other, that it demands a new set of eyes each time.

That happens by attempting to see with the eyes of every side.

"I was trying to describe it to her, and she was like, 'I think you're depressed'—and a light bulb went off. 'Is that what this is?' I just thought the world was heavy and no one was sharing the weight."[12]
— Baron Vaughn

---

[11] The DSM (Diagnostic and Statistical Manual of Mental Disorders) is now in its fifth iteration, and has recently been slated for incremental changes á la software revisions, such as 5.1, 5.2, and so on.

[12] John Moe interviewing Baron Vaughn, "8: Baron Vaughn and His Inadvisable All-Cheerio Diet," *The Hilarious World of Depression*. American Public Media. Podcast audio, Jan. 30, 2017

Pushing Past
the Birth Pains of Dialogue

Here's where we are.

- Those with depression can describe what it's like with similar images and vocabulary.

- We are, however, quick to dismiss depression. We invalidate mental illness because *we're wired not to fathom* the depth of such mental battles. We instead leap to "easier" conclusions, leading to mockery or indifference.

- Depression itself will hit a threshold of unknowability.

So what can we do? How do we communicate better?

For those without depression (or for those like me who are quick to be suspicious)—

My utmost exhortation is that **we're aware of our temptation towards dismissal**. Plain and simple: many of us are wired to be biased. If we consider the complexity of depression, it's an uphill battle to offer grace. When we can first recognize the obstacles that stop us from connecting, then we're on our way to healing—and that's part of the fight towards understanding.

Fortunately, it's very possible to widen our heuristics. *Empathic concern* is a complex process that develops later in life, but the brain can actually be trained to get better at it, like learning a musical instrument or a second language.[13] We can practice pausing to investigate and to offer empathy. It happens "when deliberate attempts are made to take the perspective of the target person."[14] This is *perspective-taking*.[15] Without it, our dialogue is sunk.

My hope is that you may hit **slow-motion** and rotate these experiences in all their dimensions, that there's a willingness to **validate** more than to criticize, and that there's an **awareness** of our capacity for prejudice.

For those who are fighting depression (and for those who seek to understand) —

The bad news is that we will never find the perfectly ideal person to hear us. When someone says, "I understand what you're going through" — can anyone *really* understand what someone's going through?

I must remind myself that we're each never fully understood, and if we each have a unique mosaic of signs and symptoms, *then we must not be too angry if our depression is at first dismissed.* We must not instantly consider the other person morally wrong or a "bad listener" or "one of *those* people." Though the initiative should not be on us for others

---

[13] Antoine Lutz, Julie Brefczynski-Lewis, Tom Johnstone, Richard Davidson, "Regulation of the Neural Circuitry of Emotion by Compassion Meditation: Effects of Meditative Expertise," PLoS ONE, Mar 26, 2008, 3(3): e1897

[14] John R. Chambers and Mark H. Davis, "The Role of the Self in Perspective-Taking and Empathy: Ease of Self-Simulation as a Heuristic for Inferring Empathic Feelings," *Social Cognition*: Vol. 30, No. 2, Apr. 2012, pp. 153-180

[15] For more on this, watch "Brené Brown on Empathy"
https://www.youtube.com/watch?v=1Evwgu369Jw

to hear us, I hope we recognize that "this is the world we're living in," in which the everyday reflex is to judge quickly, in which conversations require more than a single shot.

If that sounds wrong to you, I agree: it's neither right nor fair. But I think it's also unfair to expect a loved one to listen with enraptured attention, especially to a murky, mishandled subject like depression. We can hopefully elevate and embrace each other's stories towards a better connection.

And if depression at its center is truly unknowable, then it was never your fault that you couldn't describe your depression. Your frustration in finding compassion will always seem like an endless quest for the missing piece of a terrible puzzle.

Every side of this discussion, then, needs help in fighting through the "unknowable void." I've noticed that when we keep attempting to connect, no matter how messy, through missteps and misunderstandings, by fits and false starts and failures—something powerful happens when we reach across the dark. Simply talking about depression out loud *and finding the words for what depression is like* is often a first step towards getting through. Not perfectly, but persistently, we can we meet in our limited, yet life-giving vocabulary of this affliction.

When our pain is exposed to light, the fear of such pain begins to lose its hold. Fear starts to shrivel the moment it is exposed. It becomes the lie that it really is.

I hope you will not hide. I hope you will find a friend you can trust and tell them what's happening inside. They might not get it. Tell them again. Or find another. And try again.

One thing I kept seeing in each survey was: "I feel better just talking about this."

We empower each other by solidifying our narratives and speaking our stories into the air. There's an immense shift internally, as if we're *taking back our power from the deep*, and of course, in knowing that we're not alone.

"In each of my friends there is something that only some other friend can fully bring out. By myself I am not large enough to call the whole man into activity; I want other lights than my own to show all his facets."[16]

— C.S. Lewis

---

[16] C.S. Lewis, *The Four Loves* (NY: HarperOne, 1960, 2017) p. 78

If you're either at the edge of depression or thinking of harming yourself right now, please don't hesitate to call a friend. If they don't answer, leave a long message. You might be surprised that it helps. Also, I love you, dear friend, and you are loved.

Chapter 2
Moving at a Dead Stop

Disclaimer: This chapter contains some intense imagery about depression and might be a trigger. I advise skipping if you are currently struggling.

Volition to Change

"Nowhere," I tell him.

"What do you mean?" he asks.

"I'm just ... nowhere. And somewhere else. Like the thing with Zeno's arrow. Moving at a dead stop."

The therapist nods, making another note across his desk, *click*, his pen, *click*, a scribble, jot, a bird singing outside, *click*, the therapist talking but I'm watching this puffed-up bird sing, *click*, I can see the therapist writing, *Anxiety, manic, dependency, prone to grandeur and hyperbole, of no volition to change, typical teen angst common for his age.*

I'm on the ground. A freshman. A bottle rolls off my chest. Some of the beer spills out, innards across my shirt, trickling down my ribs, *clink*, the bottle hits the tile and rolls, stops at a groove, *clink*, and I'm waiting for the beer to kick in so I can feel something, anything, and I hear my stepmom throw something across the kitchen at my dad, a microwave, and it beeps its very last beep, muffled and resigned.

I'm in the car. Parked on campus, sixth year of college.

I look down. I have a pen cap and I'm trying to open my wrists, frantic scrawls in fast diagonals, yet methodically somehow, and I'm not really sure why but tears have carved my face into my jeans and I'm actually laughing, and it feels tight in my stomach, like a knot tied up through my lungs, but I keep flailing with this pen cap, which isn't working, and suddenly it's working, and crimson splashes my pants and I quietly wrap my jacket around my wrist and I drive with one hand to go home.

I'm at the bottom of the stairs. Looking up. Sixth month of marriage. I imagine floating at the top of the staircase, my neck askew, feet off the ground, *creak,* and I'm nowhere and everywhere, two places at once, Schrödinger's joke, *croak,* a rope in one hand and a note in the other, and I get this flash of my mom calling me *stupid* and my dad calling me never, and I walk away from the stairs and lie down on the floor under the side of the coffee table and I remember being fifteen again and I shut my eyes hard enough to see stars.

I'm at a cafe. Check-out. I'm not sure when; it's after church service, I think, or before work, and the cashier asks what I want and I'm smiling, but the sides of my lips are cutting into my cheeks and I don't remember how I got here and I look around and see people laughing and talking and browsing their phones and sipping their lattes like they really mean it, and you know, I really want that, but I've forgotten how to do these kinds of things, and the cashier asks what I'd like again, and I turn and drop my phone and keys and wallet in one swooping crash, and my hands are not shaking but I am.

Only a moment before, it was all fine. A moment after, I see the tail end of myself rush down the abyss with the rest of me. Imagine a quivering hole in your guts, and pull at one loose thread of your three pound brain down that hole, faster until friction melts away your stomach lining, faster as your brain-thread bumps along the charred edges, faster until you are left with a gutted chassis where echoes cease to return. It's senseless horror.

"What does that mean?" I ask the therapist. I'm back across the desk, the bird knocking at the window.

"Does what mean?" he asks.

"*No volition to change.*"

The therapist draws back his notes with a sharpened hiss. "How did you see that? You can't peek, that's not acceptable."

"But what does it mean? I'm not judging you, I just want to know, please."

"It means—" and he stops himself. "It means only I can ask the questions here, okay? I ask and you tell, this is a safe place where you can be yourself, okay?"

"Volition?" I ask, scratching my temple. "Like, willpower?"

"Mr. Park," he says, "let's call it a day."

"So I just need willpower, right? Can you please tell me how? I'll do anything not to be like this, I'll do the volition thing, please, I can do that."

"I need your help," I tell my senior pastor.

I'm in a meeting with the pastor and two other elders, begging to take a break from ministry. I'm the youth pastor in an Asian-American church, one of the biggest in the city. A week before the meeting, one hour before I had to preach for worship service, I had a breakdown at the door of my house. I turned the knob, fell over, and couldn't find my breath. I tried not to weep but I wept and wept and wept, all over the floor, and as much as I tried to pass the threshold, I could not step out of my house.

Now I'm in the senior pastor's lobby, a tight square of a room with closed curtains and empty walls, the plastic wrap still choking the couches.

The pastor removes his glasses. "What help?" he asks.

"I think ... I think I need a break. A long break."

He draws his head back, bemused. "Why?" he asks.

"I just want to die. I want to kill myself."

"Why?" he asks again. "What for?"

"It's nobody's fault, it's just my own problem."

At the words, "It's just my own problem," the senior pastor perks up.

"You're right," he says. "You've been a problem. Do you know how stressed I've been because of you? Do you know the shame you wrought to this office?"

"I know, and I'm very sorry." I bow my head. "You don't have to give me a break. I can resign, too. I just don't want to die."

The senior pastor has that puzzled look on his face again, and then he looks out the window and *laughs*.

He says, "What do you want to die for? Is everything so bad? Do you think you work so hard to be so depressed?"

I nod and nod. I believe everything he says. *I'm so stupid to be like this. I'm an idiot, an idiot. I'm just a big drain on the church.*

But some other part of me thinks, *Is this really okay? Can't we find some better way to talk about this?*

"How long?" he asks, shaking his head.

"Is two months acceptable? Is that—"

"Two months!" he roars. "I've been doing this for twenty-five years, and I've never been so lucky."

I look at the floor. "I'm sorry, I can—"

"Fine," he says. "You take two months. Get better. And listen: don't tell anyone why you're taking this break. Don't say the word *depression*. Don't ever say it. We'll say you have a physical health issue. That will go over better with the others. No one can know you're weak like this, or they won't trust you with their children. You are not depressed. You are away."

I'm in the hospital. Twenty-one. I've swallowed half a bottle of extra strength acetaminophen. My brother is there. He says, "That must've been a hell of a headache," and we both laugh. I love that sound. In the middle of laughing, I vomit all over the place. It's pitch black. The nurse had given me a cup of liquid charcoal to neutralize the pills in my stomach. It's blasting out of my nostrils; my body is ejecting a nightmare. My brother scrambles back from his chair and he grabs someone to help. I try to tell him I'm okay, but more vomit comes out. I think the stuff is working though. My liver doesn't feel like it's twisting into my ribs.

I'm in a mental institution, one of those white-wall lock-ups with the words "Life" or "Care" or "Point" in the title. I've been discharged from the hospital after three days, and I have to be Baker Act'ed (the nurses keep saying it that way like a verb, "You've been Baker Act'ed"). I've lost thirteen pounds since I first got to the hospital. My bunkmate is this guy who thinks roaches are inside the floorboards and crawling into his pores. Everyone keeps rolling eyes at him.

We're at a group meeting with a dozen patients and the counselor asks, "What's your goal today?" and we have these giant rubber pens with round sheets of paper. One of the guys jumps out the door and pulls the fire alarm and starts yelling, "I don't care, I'll suck it for crack, I'll keep working them corners for crack, this is a free country!" Two nurses sedate him. We hear the guy being dragged across the floor, sneakers scraping the linoleum, his shrieks drowned out by the alarm.

The counselor asks again, "What's your goal today?"

I write down, *To get out.*

Later that night, my bunkmate wakes me up. He's spinning his mattress over his head in circles, saying, "Roaches in my bed, my veins, come on, come on, it's true, it's really true!"

I step toward him and hold his mattress still. "Hey," I say. "I know. Let's look for them, you know? If we don't find any, we can sleep, how's that? Let's look for them together."

He likes this plan so we get on our hands and knees at three in the morning and look for roaches. It takes about thirty seconds and he plops onto his mattress and goes right back to sleep.

I try to pray for him. I can't imagine how hard it must be for this guy, to really think roaches are slithering in his veins right now. Never mind that it isn't true. It was true for him.

I'm sorry, I say. *I'm sorry it hurts so bad. I'm sorry, man. At least you can sleep tonight. God, be here somehow.*

I'm counseling someone in the back row of church after service. I'm a pastor with depression, like the start of a bad bar joke. This girl tells me she wants to die. I ask her, "How come?" She says, "I feel this way all the time. A sort of *hum* underneath everything. But it's not a feeling. There's no feeling. It's a constant nothing."

I nod. "Like you're nowhere, and somewhere else."

"Yes," she says. "Something like that. I mean, I got it good. I have no reason to be like this. My grades are fine, my parents are good, my friends get me, it's all fine. There's no reason for this"—and she bursts into tears. "There's no *reason* for any of this, really." She crumples into the pew.

I bend down to where she is.

I tell her, "I'm really sorry. It's not ... this isn't a choice, or something you did wrong. It just *is* sometimes."

"Is there ... is there a way back?" She wipes her eyes in rebellious sweeps; it doesn't help.

"Sometimes, yes," I tell her. "Not always. It's more like, there's no going back to how it was, but only going toward a different kind of normal. But a not-normal normal."

She laughs between tears. "That sounds *terrible*, really terrible."

"I want to say it gets better or something, or there's a right combination of words for this, but it's not like that. It's a climb uphill through a swamp and the tide is against you. But the climb, you're not alone in that. I mean, some people won't understand, and they only know what certain parts of this will look like. But you're not climbing by yourself."

"Together," she says, "is what I need right now. That's *all* I need right now."

And we pray: *God, be here somehow.*

Chapter 3
Everyone's Got Advice

"Cheer Up, Buddy!"

You're going to find very quickly that when you're depressed, nearly **everyone's got advice for you**. Everyone thinks they know what's best and what you *ought* to do.

It's well-intentioned, and it's not all bad—but in that very moment, when you're in the colorless fog, those motivational one-liners are often tacky, tone-deaf, and untenable.

If depression robs you of your ability to logically comprehend and make sense of life, then any advice or solution is not going to reach into the heart of depression.

So what can we do?

My hope here's to give a voice to those who have been depressed, so they can share in their own words what they have found helpful and what they have most definitely not. In a sense, this is *advice about the advice.*

One of the survey questions I asked was:

Which parts of the conversation around depression really bother you?

Some of the respondents wrote:

> The "Just Cheer Up" and "Exercise!" and "Give it to God."
> Also, "My brother's mother in law's sister's son took this
> woo supplement and it was a miracle!"

I hated guilt-trip talks like, "What about your parents, don't you feel guilty putting them through this?"

I've been told I was selfish, that I need to think about what I'm grateful for so that my mood would brighten.

Regardless of their intentions (which are usually good, of course), I wish more people would have the maturity to just acknowledge they don't know much about it.

I dislike having to justify my depression because I don't always display symptoms of depression. If I have a good day or if I'm able to laugh or seem happy, I find people often think that my depression isn't a real illness, or that I can simply have a positive attitude and it will go away. I have good days and bad days, but it is still always there, just like any other chronic illness.

Conversations about depression tend to be either dismissive or coddling, not much of a real balance. I think what aggravates me the most is the "Oh, I totally understand" conversation. No, no you don't. It's actually great that you don't; I wouldn't wish this on anyone.

I think trying to combat depression with 100% positivism has more damaging results than good. By positivism I mean, "Try to look at the bright side of things always," or, "Focus on being happy and things that make you happy," or, "Always be positive." It's not a new thought, but it makes suffering, heaviness or darkness not allowed to be real, valid parts of the story. So now I'm "off" and feel even worse about being "off."

Religious people tend to tell me I'm not trusting God/praying enough; non-religious people tend to tell me that I'm just not trying hard enough to be positive.

I hate when people ask me, "Why don't you just trust God?" or even worse if they say, "If you have an eternal joy, how can you be sad and depressed?" Like it's a switch and you're either joyful or depressed. I believe joy and depression can co-exist.

People try to point out really obvious things that I know but cannot do at a specific moment in time.

They tell you that it's just God growing you into a stronger person.

The Church isn't talking about mental illness. We have amazing secular organizations fighting stigma—and I absolutely love it. But what are we as Christians doing to help those who are hurting? A sermon on God's love won't do the trick. As much as I adore God and love Scripture, a Bible quote isn't going to do the trick. We need hearts poured out for each other. We need true and authentic encounters.

On a Reddit forum, a Redditor attempts to give motivational advice about depression, writing:

"Remember that you have absolute power in your life and you can change it however you want."

Another Redditor wisely replies:

> "I understand you may be trying to be helpful, but I've seen this response all over the internet and in real life as well. I get that your sentiments are genuine ... but fixing the situation isn't simply a problem of 'getting motivated.' Mental illness in its uglier forms can and does rob people of the capacity to lead healthy lives. A visit to any psychiatric hospital will confirm the existence of the absolutely insane amounts of sadness the human mind has the capacity to suffer under. Depression is real and not something that can be willed away by better diet and sunlight. Yes, these things may *help*, but realize that 1.) these things will not instantly cure, and 2.) even the thought of taking these steps can be too much to ask for someone in the throes of depression."[17]

A Coat Made of Sugar

I want to make sure I'm not saying, "Never say anything." We do need advice to expand our options. I'd hate for the depressed person to get bitter any time someone tries to help. I'd hate for the friend of a depressed person to constantly second-guess themselves when they open their mouths.

---

[17] "I want to die, but I don't want to kill myself. Please share your thoughts and opinions," *Reddit*, Feb. 17, 2013, edited for length
https://www.reddit.com/r/depression/comments/18ozz6/i_want_to_die_but_i_dont_want_to
_kill_myself/

But bad advice is not benign, and can become downright disastrous.

I remember a particular megachurch in which the pastor (an Asian-American; too close to home) constantly preached that "emotion is a prison" and that "we're called to be dead to feelings." He used the Bible verses about being "dead to the world" and "dead to sin" to support his case. The pastor, a surprisingly emotional person, claimed that depression was a "sin" and "self-centered" because it focused on all the negatives of life instead of "rejoicing in Christ"—the same Christ, by the way, who wept at death, yelled at the corrupt, and begged God to spare him from being crucified.

I've seen the devastating effects of such moralistic preaching. One of the church attenders, a young Asian-American woman, messaged me through social media, saying how awful she felt all the time about "not being dead enough."

The institutional church culture appears to have the least tact with depression. It often sends off sufferers with vapid platitudes. You may have heard clichés like, "God is using this to teach you a lesson" or, "This is God's Will" or, "Everything happens for a reason." You may have heard that anxiety is "not trusting God" or that even sickness means "you need more faith." At church, I've heard a billion times: "Pray more, read more Bible, confess your sin, cast out the devil, claim your promises." As recently as this week, I received a message from a self-professed Christian who wrote, "Your depression is demonic. Tell it to leave and it will leave. Jesus didn't die so you can go through this. I went through severe depression for three years and God took it away completely. Stop, suck it up and tell satan to leave."

I'm glad this worked for him. But for many of us: this, my friends, is not how depression works.

I think most Christians get caught up by this idea that they need to look like they have an answer for everything or else their faith is at stake. The stronghold of "certainty" is such a big deal in religious circles because "knowing more" usually means being devout and faithful. Saying "I don't know what to say" is like a death sentence to so many of us, but really, I'd be relieved if more just admitted, "I don't know how to do this" and were open to learning.

For a person with depression, there's this almost two-prong battle of handling the dark inside and then handling other peoples' responses and perceptions. That gets really old, really fast.

I have to apologize here for religious folks like me, who offered quick fixes with good intentions but fell short with shrill slogans. I'm sure I've done it, too. Even if such theology or advice is true, I have hardly *ever* seen this pull anyone from the edge at their very worst moment. They're fine suggestions if they help, but in the end, they impose a secondary pressure for the hurting person. It adds the burden of a religious checklist. And there's no way I'd ever endorse that a magical prayer or "more faith" is going to cure depression, as if just enough religion will set you right.

It's easy to go hard on the church here, but I've found that secular "pop culture" doesn't do any better. Secular solutions actually operate from the same false "religious" mechanism.

Pop culture elevates *power-positive thinking,* so that all you have to do is "cheer up, stop being negative, focus on what's good, drink this herbal tea, try this breathing technique." Again, these are sensible tips if they help, but in the end, entirely trite and wearisome for those who are depressed.

Barbara Ehrenreich, a breast cancer survivor, writes on how positive thinking absolutely exhausted her during her cancer. In her book, *Bright-Sided: How the Relentless Promotion of Positive Thinking Has Undermined America* (quite a snappy title), she makes the case that "the failure to think positively can weigh on a cancer patient like a second disease." She continues:

> "Breast cancer, I can now report, did not make me prettier or stronger, more feminine or spiritual. What it gave me, if you want to call this a 'gift,' was a very personal, agonizing encounter with an ideological force in American culture that I had not been aware of before—one that encourages us to deny reality, submit cheerfully to misfortune, and blame only ourselves for our fate."[18]

---

[18] Barbara Ehrenreich, *Bright-Sided: How the Relentless Promotion of Positive Thinking Has Undermined America* (NY: Mertropolitan Books, 2009) pp. 43-44

All this places the burden on the sufferer.[19] At best, I want to believe that those who are quick to give advice want to offer *something,* and are trying to close a "discrepancy of helplessness." Or maybe saying *nothing* means we don't care, so we must speak into the void. But I think these motives, as good as they sound, might reveal an even deeper problem.

> *"... I see people, as they approach me, trying to make up their minds whether they'll 'say something about it' or not. I hate if they do, and if they don't."*[20]
> — C.S. Lewis

I Can't Handle the Me that I See in You

Here's the hard truth.

Both the church culture and pop culture endorse a sort of "powering through" because it really translates to, *"I don't have time to get involved with your struggle."* What's usually being said is: "Pray more and be positive *so I don't have to deal with you.*"

Theology and wisdom have their place, but I suspect that we rush the hurting past their hurt *because it hurts too much to*

---

[19] The "It Gets Better" project, a response to LGBT teen suicides, was shown to negatively affect coping mechanisms and *increase* depression. Russell B. Toomey, Caitlin Ryan, Rafael M. Diaz, and Stephen T. Russell, " Coping with Sexual Orientation-Related Minority Stress," *Journal of Homosexuality,* Apr. 25, 2017

[20] C.S. Lewis, *A Grief Observed,* (NY: Seabury Press, 1961) p. 10

sit in their furnace. It's a kind of **reverse projecting**: I can't bear to look into my own uncertainty when I see yours.

My urge to offer advice has good intentions, *but it's also a way to offload the hard work of navigating the wound with the wounded. I offer a reason of certainty because it's easier than traveling with the hurting in the uncertainty. It's a way to protect myself from answering the unanswerable. I don't like the silence because it makes* **me** *uncomfortable. I have to offer something or else it makes* **me** *feel helpless.*

It's the same reflex that happens when some of us see someone cry. "Don't cry," we might say, even though very often, crying is the only way to heal through the river of all we have held inside. I've found that *when I say, "Don't cry," that's about protecting me from discomfort rather than leaning into your hurt and healing.*

So all my advice makes your pain, your tragedy, and your depression about insulating *me* instead of moving towards you. You can do one from the rooftops, but the other means diving into the smells and groans of their misery.

It's dirty. It's work. And no one naturally wants to pay the high cost of navigating someone's pain.

> *"The frequent attempt to conceal mental pain increases the burden: it is easier to say 'My tooth is aching' than to say 'My heart is broken.'"*[21]
> — C.S. Lewis

---

[21] C.S. Lewis, *The Problem of Pain* (NY: HarperCollins, 1940, 1996) p. 161

"You're Not Alone: You Have Me"

I also asked in the survey:
What kind of dialogue have you found helpful?
Respondents wrote:

> Honest, non-judgmental conversations about emotions and feelings that are hard to describe.

> Just being there to answer questions of doubt, being there in the middle of the night to pray with me over the phone. I find it helpful when people ask questions or just actually engage in the conversation rather than take this quiet, "hands-off" approach where they're too afraid to say anything at all. The connection helps far more than silence or pat "I'm sorrys".

> When people tell me I can feel this way, I can let myself bleed for a little while. Good friends have tried to look at the root of what's causing it, or have gently led me to really think and talk through what it is that I think and feel, and have tried to find the truths which oppose my harmful thoughts.

> I love the quote by Rachel Held Evans that says, "People bond more over shared brokenness than shared beliefs." I found so much healing in raw conversation about the nitty, gritty, painful parts of life. Healing in the honest "I don't know but I'm sorry it feels that way, or happened that

way." I found the "me too" helpful. I also found it helpful when people asked if they could suggest something, rather than telling me how to deal with it. And dialogue in which someone asks about it more than once, rather than hearing about it once and never asking again, which further perpetuates the feeling that *no one really wants to hear about it.*

Dialogue that is helpful usually involves some amount of both tips for how to break out of a funk as well as supportive statements letting those with depression know they're just as valuable as someone who doesn't have depression.

I can tell when someone genuinely cares and takes the time to talk with me about it; even if they make suggestions that don't or haven't worked, just knowing that they care enough to invest in me means the world.

One sister I knew would periodically text me Bible verses of encouragement and honestly, in those depressed moments, every little thought counted.

I have found people asking questions like, "How can I be of support?" or "What has been going on in your life?" to be helpful. I find those types of questions to be genuine. I don't expect people to have answers or solutions, but it's really helpful when the dialogue is intentional, and the other person is providing words of affirmation.

I find that words of encouragement and praise help me, even if I don't think it's true, and even if they're only saying that to make me feel better. One powerful phrase that always consoles me is, *"You're not alone, you have me."*

Saying, "I'm just so glad you told me." "I'm so glad and honored to share this space with you." "I really want to be a part of your life in any way, so how can I help?"

The common thread that I kept seeing in these replies was for a friend to be *curious*. To ask how to help.

Even perfect advice can have bad timing. And what's helpful for some is not for others. Some wanted the advice; for some, presence. For some, the Bible or a book; for some, music, or silence, or a party. Or as one respondent said, *I want them to ask questions ... I want the curiosities to come out. I want to relay the truths.*

Just asking can be enough.

I Say: Say Nothing

I've often been asked:

"What do you say to someone who's just tried to attempt suicide?" I'm guessing they ask me because, well, I've tried to attempt suicide.

And I think that's the wrong premise.

What do you say?

I say: say nothing.

I wonder if, rather than reasons or theology or pep talk, we can offer a microphone.

To give the depressed person a voice, even if that voice says, *"What I feel is: I feel nothing."*

Maybe you *were* given a microphone, but you had to proclaim, "Everything happens for a reason" and "But God—!" and other such clichés because that's what you were supposed to say, to be a "good witness," to show off a rock-star faith, to look strong and stable, to end on a hopeful note despite dying inside. There's a subtle pressure not to be a *downer* in public places, especially if you're a leader—because no one seems to know how to respond to the awkward limbo of unresolved pain.

For me, that's a good thing. No one *has* to respond. I don't need your perfect reply. Saying *nothing* is sometimes the very thing I need. I don't need the rescue. I don't need the Type-A Fixer. I'm grateful for such persistence—but even the very best are still overbearing, as if the right set of words could crack me open.

Sometimes I just want the space for someone to hear me out, even if that means I say nothing at all.

Sometimes that means hamburgers, ice cream, Netflix, loud music, green tea, and bringing your dog over.

One of the most invaluable gifts to me from my community was being able to express or *not* express myself around others, however I needed to vent—without someone on their platform telling me what they thought I "ought" to do.

*Can you just sit here with me, without saying a single word —
and let me be depressed?*

I need *you*, and you being here's not nothing.

—

I called a friend once, when I was on the edge, and I had
one request.

*"Can you stay on the phone with me while I do my laundry?
And just not say anything? I mean, you can breathe really loud or
clear your throat or something, so I know you're there. Just let me
know you're there."*

And that was all I needed.

*"One of the things we do sometimes in the face of very difficult con-
versations is we try to make things better. [But] if I share something
with you that's very difficult, I'd rather you say, 'I don't even know
what to say right now. I'm just so glad you told me.' Because the truth
is, rarely can a response make something better. What makes something better is connection."*[22]
— Brené Brown

*"Then [Job's friends] sat on the ground with him
for seven days and seven nights.
No one said a word to him,
because they saw how great his suffering was."*
— The Book of Job, 2nd chapter, verse 13

---

[22] Brené Brown, "Brené Brown on Empathy," 2:14-2:38. Dec. 10, 2013
https://www.youtube.com/watch?v=1Evwgu369Jw

Part 2
The Flashback

Record Scratch, Freeze-Frame:
"You're Probably Wondering
How I Got Here"
(And So Am I)

A microscope over the science,
culture, and psychology
around depression,
that the parts would
inform the whole.

"You Brought This on Yourself" vs. "You Couldn't Help Yourself"

In the hospital, I occasionally get shadowed by a student nurse so that they can observe the duties of a chaplain. Most people, no matter how much theology they know, have little idea what a chaplain does.

"I pictured a hooded, bald white man with a rope around his waist," Audrey said, "or a collared priest type, very somber and sour."

Audrey was a student nurse from Scotland. She was part of a foreign exchange program that toured the highest-rated hospitals in America. I felt a bit proud of my hospital, but also sharply self-conscious about her expectations.

"Sorry," I told Audrey, "I've seen all five seasons of *Breaking Bad* and I like weightlifting and I have a Facebook. I'm also Asian. Pretty weird, huh?"

"So you don't live in a cave six days a week to preach on the seventh?" she said, laughing loudly while I waited. "Sorry," she said, still laughing, "Scotland is not very religious and we don't see many of you. I can't imagine we'd call a prie—I mean a chaplain for anything."

Audrey mentioned she was specializing in mental health in her nursing program, and in Scotland, the science around it was entirely rooted in the patient's upbringing, environment, and past trauma. In other words, Audrey was trained in the social model of depression, in which it was seen as a condition caused by external factors. That meant her training back home was more thoughtful and holistic than my own; she was essentially time-traveling backwards by visiting a hospital in America.

"I know in the States that mental illness is seen as the sovereign choice of the individual," she said in her colorful Scottish brogue. "Americans see mental illness as a choice, do they not?"

We were on the way to our first patient, a heroin addict who was almost brain-dead. His parents had asked for counsel from a chaplain; they were upset, grieving, and bewildered that their son had "done this to himself."

"Mostly yes," I replied. "In the States we have this idea that nearly everything that happens to a person is their fault, or if they have a mental illness, they can power through it. 'Pull yourself up by the bootstraps' and all that. Eastern-Asians like me have the same sort of mentality, an honorable work ethic, or something cosmic, like karma."

"Ah," Audrey said, raising her fist, "we are years ahead then. All our facilities just *know* that an addict or the mentally ill or even a *murderer* was shaped by social stimuli."

"I agree completely," I said. "If I grew up with the same set of circumstances, that place, their time, their trauma, I probably would have made the same choices."

"Yes!" Audrey said, breathing hard. "An individual is not their choices! Oh, not at all. They are much more."

Audrey continued, explaining that a person's choices are as far from a person as the east is from the west, and that our personalities are shaped by a mixed cauldron of unseen forces. We spoke about the hospital, the prison system, the distribution of wealth and welfare, substance abuse: and in all these cases, Audrey was absolutely certain that individuals were carried along by the winds of higher establishment. The prosperous are lucky and the less fortunate have been victimized.

In Scotland, she kept saying, *we help those who cannot help themselves.*

We arrived to the patient, Kevin, who was sitting lopsided in a chair with a mark of dried saliva on his left side, one eye closed and one eye staring aimlessly. His parents both stood up; Kevin's mother had been on a makeshift bed, the father staring out the window in the corner.

I introduced myself and Audrey, and we listened to their story about Kevin's decline. His parents couldn't understand why Kevin had gone down this path: he was a bright, gifted child who had attended a wealthy magnet school, played on the basketball team all four years of high school, had a black belt in Karate, dated the same person for six years, and had a scholarship for the first two years of college—until he lost it when his GPA took a nosedive.

"He admitted to us the first time he tried marijuana," Kevin's mother said, "and we were fine with it. The next month, he OD'ed on heroin. This is the second time ... and I don't think he's coming back."

Kevin's father stomped on the floor with his foot, then shuddered into tears. "Why? Why, chaplain? We did everything right!"

Suddenly Audrey leaned forward and asked, "Have you ever heard of EFT? Emotional Freedom Technique?"

Kevin's parents both jumped. "No," one said, looking away. "Nope," the other said, looking back at me, shrugging.

"Ah, well," Audrey said, bright and cheery, "EFT was developed to reduce stress and it requires you to just tap your forehead in various places until you feel a thousand percent better!" She proceeded to demonstrate, and she struck her own forehead with two fingers, not quietly. "Like this, you see? Studies have proven it decreases stress and I know you'll find it useful."

There was a long, long silence. Then Kevin's mother looked back at me and said, "So anyway, that's where we're at. Can you pray for us?"

On our exit, I asked Audrey in the elevator, "Just wondering, Audrey: what made you think of EFT?"

Audrey, still as cheerful as she was in the room, said, "Oh, I've just read a study on the EFT technique and I thought it might work for them. I personally don't believe in it myself, but I thought it would be appropriate for them."

I was confused. *For all of Audrey's talk about mental illness being a social condition, which I agreed with, Audrey had offered a technique to "fix" a distressed mother.*

I thought of a hundred different responses and I restrained myself from all of them. Instead I asked, "Was there something in their story that moved something in your story to offer a technique for them?"

What I expected Audrey to say was, *"Yes, their story seemed so unsolvable and hopeless that I was most likely projecting my own discomfort towards an unfixable situation by offering a practical fix-it formula that I don't even believe in to ease the unresolved dissonance in myself."*

She instead said, "The studies show that it works."

Where There's Smoke: Tracking Prometheus in a World on Fire

Audrey and I were brushing up against a classic dilemma: the debate between seeing mental illness as a *choice* versus a *disease*. It's a debate also seen with addiction, alcoholism, gambling, and body size—and unfortunately, like many issues, has been politicized between liberal and conservative dichotomies. "Choice" is seen as a fundamentalist, right-wing moralism while "disease" is seen as a pampered, bleeding-heart free-for-all.

Maybe this debate shouldn't matter. Isn't it just abstract and fruitless ideological chest-thumping?

I believe, though, that this discussion matters because *the way we perceive the cause of mental illness will limit or expand our approach.* A wrong perception can lead to the wrong treatment. If your car is speeding, it makes a difference to know whether you're driving too fast or your brakes have been cut. If your leg is in pain, it helps to know whether it's from a bruise, a break, or a blood clot.

The cost of misinformation is high. In the 1840s, Dorothea Dix petitioned for the first reforms in American "mental asylums," where those with mental illnesses (called "the insane") were imprisoned alongside violent criminals. Today, there are ten times more people with mental illnesses in American prisons than in hospitals.[23] Very little has changed.

My hope here's to chart a course through *choice* and *disease*, to peel back layers of **myths** and to stitch together a better **truth**. We'll look at the **science behind depression**, which can defang some of the mystery and reduce fear on all sides. Truly, the more you know, the more empowered you'll become to *find* help and *to* help.

For the rest of the chapter, I'll lay out some important data about our views on depression, then draw these in towards a *third way* beyond choice and disease. I highly welcome disagreement as you read along, but I hope you read to the end before tossing the book, as I will eventually disagree with myself.

In my exhaustive exploration of depression, I found at least three dimensions for the *root cause*. The first two views see depression as a "disease" and the third sees it as a "choice."[24]

1) Biological: A genetic predisposition or a physiological event, such as brain damage or a thyroid issue. When you hear that "depression is a disease," it's mostly referring to the biological cause.

2) Social: External factors like family of origin, childhood trauma, socioeconomic class, stress, or loss. This is a newer idea to emerge in the last few decades.

3) Psychological: A view of the self, emerging from a myriad of factors like self-image, behavioral patterns, and coping mechanisms.

The most popular view today is to see depression as a *biological disease*, or what has classically been called a *chemical*

---

[24] There's yet a fourth cause, the *spiritual*, but we will save this discussion for the final chapters of the book.

imbalance. The opposing view, that "depression is a choice," has become more appalling and unacceptable in medical circles.

However, it's not that simple.

Right off the bat: The chemical imbalance theory, once a darling in psychiatry, has mostly been debunked as the sole issue. It's not that biology isn't the cause, but that there may be a cause *to* the biological cause. Imagine again a car that has an engine problem: how did it get that way? It's true that the brain *can* have a "chemical imbalance," a manufacturer's defect, perhaps, but it's not the *sole* cause of mental illness, and it still doesn't explain the *why*. Andrew Scull, a professor of sociology at the University of California, writes:

> "A simplistic biological reductionism increasingly ruled the psychiatric roost. Patients and their families learned to attribute mental illness to faulty brain biochemistry, defects of dopamine, or a shortage of serotonin. It was biobabble as deeply misleading and unscientific as the psychobabble it replaced, but as marketing copy it was priceless."[25]

Actor and comedian Stephen Fry, in his documentary *The Secret Life of the Manic Depressive,* explained the reasons for his mental illnesses as solely biological, but Richard Bentall,

---

[25] Andrew Scull, "A psychiatric revolution," *The Lancet*, Vol. 375, Iss. 9722, Apr. 10, 2010, pp. 1246 - 1247

professor of psychology at Liverpool University, wrote a measured response:

> "Conventional psychiatry tends to decontextualise psychiatric disorders, seeing them as discrete brain conditions that are largely genetically determined and barely influenced by the slings and arrows of misfortune ... **According to this 'brain conditions' view, psychiatric disorders occur largely out of the blue in individuals who are genetically vulnerable, and the only appropriate response is to find the right medication.** Even then, it is usually assumed that severe mental illnesses are life long conditions that can only be managed by continuous treatment. However, research into severe mental illness conducted over the last twenty years (not only by me, although I have contributed) tells a more complex story."[26]

Professor Bentall challenges that Stephen Fry too quickly glosses over many of the traumatic events of his own childhood, and Bentall goes on to cite dozens of sources that *there's a link between trauma and the shape of a depressed person's brain.* There's visible proof that people with depression have shrunken gray matter. It's absurd to say that a particular brain size invited the trauma. Rather, trauma most likely impacted the brain in such a way that the brain is predisposed to depression.

---

[26] Richard Bentall, "All in the Brain?" *Canterbury Christ Church University,* February 19, 2016. Bold emphasis mine.

This means that depressive episodes *can* occur from biology and "out of the blue"—but the biology was perhaps first set into motion by external causes.

Bentall makes the case that **the reason an episode of depression occurs in the first place can usually be traced back to what we have been through**. It's too cut-and-dry to say that *all* who fight depression are hapless prisoners to their biology. The phrase "chemical imbalance" has monopolized the conversation for too long.

Clinicians now tend to think that depression is more like an omelette, composed of at least the three mentioned ingredients: biological, social, and psychological. Each ingredient can affect the other, which then reacts right back.

A person who is more genetically predisposed to depression (ingredient 1: biological), could go through a depressive episode after being fired from their job (ingredient 2: social) and become worse if they're unable to cope with the job loss (ingredient 3: psychological). That same person who was genetically predisposed to depression could have experienced an unusually traumatic childhood (2: social) which could've continually linked their trauma with their self-worth (3: psych) and suffered shrinkage of certain parts of the brain (1: bio).[27] It's a complex tapestry of causes and effects, and it's difficult to discern where one factor ends and the other begins.

---

[27] Eamon McCrory, Stephanie A. De Brito, and Essi Viding, "Research review: The neurobiology and genetics of maltreatment and adversity." *Journal of Psychology and Psychiatry*, Oct. 2010, 51, 1079–1095

To only say "depression is a disease" presumes a biological vacuum in which people have almost *no other reason* for their episodes. Saying so would ignore all the traumatic social issues which are physically warping millions of brains.

Depression, then, is just as much a *social disease* as it is a biological one. The two dimensions are irrevocably linked.

Let's take a look at some of these social causes and see what we can do about them.

Brain Tattoos and Broken Highways

Audrey, our dear Scottish nurse, brought up the ACE Test, a much lesser known study now endorsed by the Center for Disease Control and Prevention. The ACE Test measures Adverse Childhood Experiences, and this score can determine your expectancy for addiction, obesity, heart disease, cancer — and yes, depression.

The ACE Test has ten yes-or-no questions, with each "yes" answer counting as one point, for a possible total of ten points. The test asks if any of the following events happened before you were an adult.[28]

Here's one of the variations of the test:

---

[28] The original ACE Study: Vincent J. Felitti, Robert F. Anda, Dale Nordenberg, David F. Williamson, Alison M. Spitz, Valerie Edwards, Mary P. Koss, James S. Marks, "Relationship of Childhood Abuse and Household Dysfunction to Many of the Leading Causes of Death in Adults," *American Journal of Preventive Medicine*, May 1998, Vol. 14, Iss. 4, pp. 245–258

1) Did a parent or other adult in the household often swear at you, insult you, put you down, or humiliate you? Or act in a way that made you afraid that you might be physically hurt?

2) Did a parent or other adult in the household often push, grab, slap, or throw something at you? Or ever hit you so hard that you had marks or were injured?

3) Did an adult or person at least five years older than you ever touch or fondle you or have you touch their body in a sexual way?

4) Did you often feel that no one in your family loved you or thought you were important or special?

5) Did you often feel that you didn't have enough to eat, had to wear dirty clothes, and had no one to protect you? Or your parents were too drunk or high to take care of you or take you to the doctor if you needed it?

6) Were your parents ever separated or divorced? Has one or more of your parents died?

7) Was your mother or stepmother often pushed, grabbed, slapped, or had something thrown at her? Or kicked, bitten, hit with a fist, or hit with something hard? Or repeatedly hit over at least a few minutes or threatened with a gun or knife?

8) Did you live with anyone who was a problem drinker or alcoholic, or who used street drugs?

9) Was a household member depressed or had a mental illness, or did a household member attempt suicide?

10) Did a household member go to prison?

These events brand themselves into children, like tattooed scars of the brain. Many of us, against our own will, are now traveling on spiritually broken highways.

If you score a four or more, your likelihood of physical and mental issues increases exponentially: depression increases by 460%, suicide by 1,220%, and those who score seven or higher on the test who *don't* drink or smoke or overeat are still 360% more likely to get heart disease than those who score a zero.[29,30] Over one of ten Americans have an ACE score of four or more.[31]

How did you do?

I scored a nine out of ten.

Give Me Something

I'm convinced that *social conditions* including trauma and upbringing are the biggest predictors of depression. If this is true, then medicine and therapy might help alleviate the symptoms of depression *but will not change the social conditions which brought about the depression in the first place.* And just as our biology is not our fault, neither are many of our social woes. They're built into the **eventualities of life.** This means it is *not* enough to simply get by on the strength of will or prescribed pills.

Allow me to pause here and say: Medicine and therapy work for many, many people, and *if it works, then it works.* Sometimes it doesn't matter how. And even if we "fix" social

---

[29] Adverse Childhood Experiences (ACEs), *Center for Disease and Control Prevention,* https://www.cdc.gov/violenceprevention/acestudy/
[30] Paul Tough, "The Poverty Clinic," *The New Yorker,* (NY: Advance, Mar. 21, 2011) pp. 25-32
[31] Calculated from a sample size of 17,421 individuals

conditions, many with mental illness will still need medication. One doesn't negate the other.

Yet medicine and therapy, despite their success rate, need to be discussed in their entire context. They can also have limited effectiveness: up to 80% of an antidepressant's effectiveness can be replicated by a placebo, and scientists are still unsure how antidepressants actually "work."[32] And about 10-30% of those with depression are resistant to treatment.[33] Therapy is also nearly equivalent to pharmaceuticals: they offer mixed results.[34]

These statistics, of course, should never stop you from seeking treatment. One saved life is enough. My concern is to tackle the whole problem. And if we include the social angle, we come up against an ethical dilemma: If someone is depressed because they're in a harmful career, marriage, or neighborhood, and then they're given antidepressants just to function in them, then it's as if *that person is being drugged to tolerate their harmful situation.* Medicine can allow you to tolerate a life that never should've been tolerated.[35]

Of course, we must be given every immediate remedy. Fixing our social situation won't magically cure depression. I

---

[32] Irving Kirsch Brett J Deacon, Tania B. Huedo-Medina, Alan Scoboria, Thomas J. Moore, Blair T. Johnson, "Initial Severity and Antidepressant Benefits: A Meta-Analysis of Data Submitted to the Food and Drug Administration," *PLOS Medicine*, 5(2): e45, Feb. 26, 2008

[33] Khalid Saad Al-Harbi, "Treatment-resistant depression: therapeutic trends, challenges, and future directions," *Patient Preference and Adherence*, May 1, 2012, Vol. 2012:6, pp. 369-388

[34] Pim Cuijpers, Marit Sijbrandij, Sander L Koole, Gerhard Andersson, Aartjan T Beekman, and Charles F Reynolds, "The efficacy of psychotherapy and pharmacotherapy in treating depressive and anxiety disorders: a meta-analysis of direct comparisons," *World Psychiatry*, Jun. 2013, 12(2), pp. 137–148

[35] A concept that I first read in *Noonday Demon* by Andrew Solomon.

again recommend every kind of help wholeheartedly (more on this in Chapter 7). My hope though is that we never stop "inspecting the factory." I hope we continually dive into the realities around us, to improve them or to prevent further damage. Social factors like poverty, dysfunctional family dynamics, a deprived education system, an unfair legal system, discrimination by race and gender, and misinformed narratives about purpose and fulfillment involve *a yet uncontrollable variable that is forced upon each person within their broken system.* And those broken systems, as you might guess, also make it impossible to get help for the very mental battles that they cause.

Author Andrew Solomon in a TEDTalk shares the story of a single mother named Lolly, who was unable to work or raise her eleven children because she was depressed. Her childhood was horrifying: she had been raped multiple times by family members and physically beaten by all the men in her life. She was too poor to reach out for resources.

Lolly happened upon a psychology professor who was doing a study on depression and the poor, and Lolly was offered a six month trial of therapy. She soon left her abusive husband, became capable of holding down a job, and experienced joy with her children again.[36,37]

---

[36] Andrew Solomon, "Case Study: The Depressed Poor; Location: Washington, D.C.; A Cure For Poverty," *The New York Times Magazine*, May 6, 2006. The name "Lolly" in this article is "Wendy," perhaps to further protect her identity.

[37] Andrew Solomon, "Depression, the secret we share | Andrew Solomon," TedxMET, The Metropolitan Museum of Art, 19:43-22:00, Dec. 18, 2013 https://www.youtube.com/watch?v=-eBUcBfkVCo

My guess is that *Lolly's social condition most likely led to her biological condition, which then perpetuated her social condition, in an unending ouroboros.*

Whether or not her depression was a "choice" or "disease," it was her social reality that prevented her from getting the help she needed.

Many of us may be locked in this same loop with no exit in sight.

Why Can't You Just—?

The stories of both "chemical imbalance" and social conditions need to be told. Yet the main problem around discussing mental illness is the same thing it's been for far too long: seeing depression as a "choice," as some kind of moral punishment. A curse.

This is especially true in the West. I believe that *Westernized culture is absolutely atrocious about the dehumanization of addicts, criminals, the homeless, and those with mental illnesses because we lay the blame completely on them.*

It happens for at least two reasons, one easy to see and the other painful to admit.

The first is that many of us make a **moral correlation** of someone's behavior with their condition. We falsely believe that someone with a mental illness must be unhealthy because there's something inherently "sick" about them. Like they haven't worked hard enough to be healthy.

Since Westernized America has always prided itself on an entrepreneurial, achievement-driven individualism, many Americans consider themselves to be self-made. If the U.S. is the "land of opportunity," this also drips with the clause, "Every man for himself." If someone has a problem, "It's not my problem; I have enough of my own." Environment and upbringing would matter less than the resolve to "rise up and be somebody." Addicts, criminals, and the homeless would've "had it coming." Success and failure, in this sort of thinking, is directly tied to effort.

This mentality is why some hesitate to count their ACE Scores or won't explore social conditions: it sounds like "I'm passing the buck" or "blaming society" for all our problems. Underneath this are the accusatory questions, "Why can't you just be happy, like I am? Why can't you just get over it, like I do? Why can't you just work hard, like me? Why can't you just—?"

All this despite the fact that *no one is a self-made person*. No one has single-handedly built their life or health or success on their own autonomy. There's too much we don't control: our genes, our era, our family, our neighborhood, and all the events that befall us. We live within pre-existing grids that largely define our opportunities.[38]

---

[38] There's evidence that those who are born to rich families and do not go to college are still two and a half times more likely to be rich than those who are born poor and *do* go to

Just as there are external factors which contribute to a person's success, I also believe the same about those who are suffering a debilitating condition.

Just as no one is a self-made millionaire, no one is necessarily a self-made addict, criminal, or person with mental illness. There are larger forces that work against the "undesirables."

Our nature is nurtured, which nurtures our nature.

—

The second reason we've fallen into a "choice" view is from a much more insidious agenda: ***Many of us simply don't want to help***. And if we can blame those with mental illnesses by saying that they're not trying hard enough, it's a free pass on our own guilt.

Nearly everyone thinks they're helpful and generous, but in my experience, *most individuals are unwilling to deal with anyone or anything that cramps their independence*. We are helpful until the very second it becomes inconvenient, or we're one-hit wonders with a single-click donation from a distance.

Online activists can pay lip service by posting courageous rants all over social media, yet at some point will drop out

---

college. Matt Breunig, " What's more important: a college degree or being born rich?" *Matt Breunig | Politics,* Jun. 13, 2013. Data from *The Pew Charitable Trusts.*

with, "I tried my best," as if to say, *"This person can't be helped."* I'm not above this either.

We leave little room for *interdependence*, the idea that our community shares both prosperity and burdens together. The urge for independence can be so strong that we will rationalize to avoid the "inconvenient."

Consider how we treat "inconvenient" groups of people. In the States, the elderly are quickly carted off to nursing homes, as opposed to other cultures' practices that generally care for the elderly.[39] It's why the homeless and criminals are seen in the States as morally repugnant and having "brought it on themselves," rather than as people who can be reformed.[40] And those with mental illnesses, including the depressed, are seen as a public nuisance, helplessly unfixable, or at worst, violently dangerous.[41]

Both my grandmother and uncle were diagnosed with schizophrenia, complete with debilitating hallucinations and paranoid delusions. Yet it was unthinkable in my own family that we'd place them in an institution. This doesn't make us better than anyone; it was simply a part of our cultural norms. And of course, there are many cases when caring for someone is impossible. In the end, my grandmother did stay in a hospice home for the last six months of her life. But as

---

[39] See Atul Gawande's *Being Mortal* about the cultural perspectives of mortality.

[40] David Buchanan, et al. "Changing Attitudes Toward Homeless People: A Curriculum Evaluation," *Journal of General Internal Medicine* 19.5 Pt 2 , May 19, 2004, pp. 566–568

[41] Angela M. Parcesepe and Leopoldo J. Cabassa, "Public Stigma of Mental Illness in the United States: A Systematic Literature Review," *Administration and policy in mental health* 40.5 (2013): 10.1007/s10488–012–0430–z. *PMC*. Web. 20 Apr. 2017.

exhausting as my grandmother and uncle could be, my family saw them as *interconnected* with us, not as an obstacle to either of my parent's independence.[42]

Many of those with mental illnesses, unfortunately, do not have the luxury of supportive family members, much less any community, who are willing to house them.

The hard part now is that if we're to have any hope of moving forward with depression, the conversation demands all of you and me. **There must be wide-scale social changes if we're to see hope for the *inconvenient*, including a movement towards *interdependence*.** Battling mental illness demands a systematic breakthrough at every level of our social climate. Each person must be woven into a web that far exceeds the individual's ability or lack of ability to fight depression.

I recognize I'm talking very idealistically. The reality is bleak. The States find it easier to continue a "containment" model that replaces rehabilitation with separation. It's a divide not much better than apartheid. Visit almost any psych facility in the States, and you'll find prison-like walls with zero direction for patients, who are sedated into zombies.[43] There's no incentive to change this. The social change we need is counterintuitive to our "freedom" and "morality." Progress will be slow.

---

[42] To be fair, many of the elderly have such declining conditions that they require professionals who are trained, paid, and can work in shifts. There comes a point when even an entire family's efforts cannot sustain care for one who has a severe illness.

[43] Lulu Miller and Alix Spiegel, "The Problem with the Solution," *Invisibilia*. National Public Radio. Podcast audio, Apr. 20, 2017

But there's reason to hope. Places like Belgium, Scotland, Canada, and Italy have seen revolutionary progress for those with mental illnesses, with an aim towards *de-institutionalization* and *integration*, even as far as back as the 1970s.[44] The afflicted in these places are not treated as inmates to be segregated, but have become woven into the social fabric, not unlike how people of different races, genders, or sexualities are becoming more accepted in the States.

While severe mental illnesses still need proper hospitalization, there are more and more countries that do not immediately isolate those with mental illnesses as if they were lepers. Visit any of the aforementioned places and you'll find the "mentally ill" who are employed, married, self-sufficient, and raising families, when they may have otherwise never been given a chance.

No, fixing society will not suddenly fix mental illness. *A healthy community doesn't automatically make a healthy brain.* Even with wide-scale social change, we still need to recognize each person in their individual struggle. We do need the option of medication and other medical treatments. But neglecting any angle—social or biological or psychological—will always leave someone behind.

—

---

[44] The Belgian city of Geel and the Italian city of Trieste have done remarkable work for people with mental illnesses.

All that to say: We've been fed the idea that depression is *only* a choice, that somehow we've chosen our way in and can choose our way out. We're inclined to deflect the burden rather than to share it. This partially explains why we're quick to find fault and "offer" advice.

Even Audrey, our dear Scottish nurse, who was raised to believe that depression was molded by systemic forces, was still not above offering a fix-it technique like EFT for stress. Sure, stress is different from depression. But I was astounded that Audrey offered a technique which *she herself did not believe would work.*

I don't question her motives; I have no doubt she wanted to help. *But a non-American who harshly criticized the American treatment of mental health was still offering an Americanized technique for mental health.* EFT itself was developed by a Stanford engineering graduate who was also an ordained minister. *It is a therapeutic method based on western independent values.*

No, Audrey does not speak for every Scot or for her side of the debate. But was Audrey unaware of the irony? That as a person who staunchly believed depression was a social disease, she was still operating on principles that saw depression as a choice?

Or was she on to something much deeper?

This leads us to one last wrinkle in the discussion.

A Prayer a Day ...

Here's the final dilemma between *choice* and *disease*.

On one hand, I don't believe that depression is a choice. There's almost nothing we can possibly do to end up with such a mental illness, and it is almost entirely branded into us by social breakdown and trauma.

On the other hand, *every single study on treating depression requires making a choice to get better.*

I believe external systemic forces are at work that hold down the depressed, *but this cannot discount the internal forces that must push back.*

This is crucial, because if we're to say, "Your mental illness is forced into you by trauma," this is an absolutely devastating life sentence on those who have been traumatized early and often. The first time I knew my ACE Score was nine points out of ten, my first question was, *Am I doomed for the rest of my life?* And on top of that, *What can I even do about all these uncontrollable social dynamics?*

The good news is that the very same researchers for the ACE Study also found a **Resilience Score**, in which positive influences and practices can rebuild you amidst trauma. These interventions unsurprisingly consisted of *interdependent connections* with constructive relationships around you (even just *one* caring relationship[45]) — but also include *personal*

---

[45] Philip A. Fisher, Megan R. Gunnar, Mary Dozier, Jacqueline Bruce, Katherine C. Pears, "Effects of therapeutic interventions for foster children on behavioral problems, caregiver

strategies like trying new things, practicing relaxation, embracing a moral compass, cognitive self-affirmation, believing in positive outcomes, renewed life purpose, and belief in a higher power.[46,47,48,49] And yes, taking medication is also part of these choices.

These practices might make you roll your eyes, but statistically, they *work.*

Take one example: A post-surgery study on patients who underwent CABG, a Coronary Artery Bypass Grafting, showed that patients who practiced private prayer had an 18% drop in post-surgery depression.[50] There are a ton of studies on CABG with similar results: meditation, music therapy, touch therapy, and relaxation techniques all can decrease wound infections, length of hospital stay, and in some cases, death. Patients who prayed could decrease their

---

attachment, and stress regulatory neural systems," *Annals of the New York Academy of Sciences,* Dec. 2006,1094, pp. 215-25.

[46] See the work and studies of Dr. Steven M. Southwick, professor of psychiatry and expert in extreme trauma and PTSD.

[47] Samoon Ahmad, Adriana Feder, Elisa J. Lee, Yanping Wang, Steven M. Southwick, Erica Schlackman, Katherine Buchholz, Angelique Alonso, Dennis S. Charney, "Earthquake impact in a remote South Asian population: psychosocial factors and posttraumatic symptom," *Journal of Traumatic Stress,* Vol. 23, No. 3, Jun. 2010, pp. 408-412

[48] Tanya N. Alim, Adriana Feder, Ruth Elaine Graves, Yanping Wang, James Weaver, Maren Westphal, Angelique Alonso, Notalelomwan U. Aigbogun, Bruce W. Smith, John T. Doucette, Thomas A. Mellman, William B. Lawson, Dennis S. Charney, "Trauma, resilience, and recovery in a high-risk African-American population," *The American Journal of Psychiatry,* Dec, 2008,165(12): pp.1566-75

[49] Adriana Feder, Samoon Ahmad, Elisa J. Lee, Julia E. Morgan, Ritika Singh, Bruce W. Smith, Steven M. Southwick, Dennis S. Charney, "Coping and PTSD symptoms in Pakistani earthquake survivors: Purpose in life, religious coping and social support," May 2013, Vol. 147, Iss. 1-3, pp. 156–163

[50] Fabio Ikedo, et al. "The effects of prayer, relaxation technique during general anesthesia on recovery outcomes following cardiac surgery," *Complementary Therapies in Clinical Practice,* May 2007, Vol. 13, Iss. 2, pp. 85–94

hospital stay by an average of two days, which would save the hospital (and you) about $4,200 per patient.[51]

I found this both deeply comforting and downright disturbing.

I found it comforting because *certain choices could actually help us through depression.* There was evidence to prove it. Yet I found it disturbing because the evidence seemed to imply, "If you don't try enough, you'll die."

This reminds me of the unhealthy Christian subculture which says, "Pray more or God won't heal you." I can't stand this sort of thing—*yet prayer scientifically helps those who are depressed and even physically injured.* Whether or not God is "activating" some kind of healing is almost beside the point: prayer and other techniques are proven to aid emotional and physical healing.

I do believe that our environment and biology play a huge role in who we are today. But there are piles of evidence which conclude that our choices have a real, tangible effect on certain conditions, including depression.[52] No matter how distasteful I find all this, I can't deny the compelling results.

I know I'm on a tightwire here, and I don't ever want to imply that you make your own bed with mental illness. We

---

[51] Charles Adam Mouch, Amanda J. Sonnega, "Spirituality and Recovery from Cardiac Surgery: A Review," *Journal of Religion and Health,* May 17, 2012, Vol. 51, No. 4, pp. 1042-1060. This is a meta-analysis of sixteen different studies, each conveying the significant results of spiritual practices.

[52] Including the cited sources above, I printed out dozens of peer-reviewed studies of how spiritual and personal practices help with depression. To cite them all would create an even more obnoxious amount of footnotes. If you'd like to follow up on this research, I recommend starting with the studies done with the military.

started this chapter saying that the psychological model of depression, the model of "choice," was the least popular and the most damning. I still agree with that assessment. But it also turns out, while the psychological model can't be used to say that depression is "your fault," it can be used to say that *you can do something about depression once you're there.*

For all of Audrey's training about mental health, she still instinctively drew on a *technique* she had learned which could manage the symptoms of stress. She didn't believe stress or mental illness was our *fault,* yet she intuitively knew that we still had to make *choices* within these conditions.

I had originally thought Audrey was projecting her own discomfort in fixing the unfixable. Maybe that was true—but what I failed to see was that she saw mental illness as a systemic issue *and* could offer evidence-based options. Despite her weird, abrupt forehead tapping, she was right: we are not without options in this battle. Maybe I was the one who was projecting my own discomfort on her. Unlike her, maybe I couldn't artfully stretch between two opposing schools of thought.

I think that Audrey, without knowing it, had helped me to merge two spheres of discourse towards an elusive *third way.*

Behind Door Number Three

One of the survey questions I asked was:

Do you feel that depression is more of a disease or a choice? Why?

Out of nearly two hundred respondents, only two people said "choice." Most answered how I would expect: a disease.

But about three-dozen respondents answered that their depression was both choice *and* a disease. It was not Either/Or, but *Both/And*.

Many still felt that choices *had* to be made in and around depression. Even if the disease was permanent and debilitating, there was a narrow window of potential choices. The respondents, perhaps without knowing it, were describing *resilience*.

I want to be careful here. I've spent some energy in this chapter showing how depression is *not* something that we choose to enter or to leave. No rational person would choose to have such a condition, and it cannot be "solved" any more than we could escape from a thousand foot pit brimming with slime.

But when our mind internally turns against us and self-sabotages during depression—*there are options that can make it worse, and some that give us a few more breaths.* The element of choice may be hijacked by our brains, which is a valid internal reality, and our social surroundings might keep us a hostage to forces beyond our control—but the door of choice is still before us, no matter how small it appears.

My bias is to dismiss any choice-driven narrative, but I've recognized that this, too, is too simplistic a view. I was confusing the *mechanism* versus the *moment*. In other words, I don't believe that depression operates on the *mechanism* of choice: no one chooses in or out. But in the *moment* of a depressive episode, we're making choices whether we want to or not.

The lie is that we will never be able to climb out of the pit no matter what we do. *The truth is that we can make choices within the pit itself.* We were probably never going to climb out of the pit in the first place, and can only decide how we survive for the next few moments before the possibility of escape.

In this sort of pit, resilience is about having a realistic view of the darkness around us while retaining a shred of light in our core being, no matter how small the light may be. It's to be pessimistic and optimistic, at the very same time.

Perhaps this is best summed up by the Stockdale Paradox, made famous by Vietnam War veteran James Stockdale, who said:

> *"You must never confuse faith that you will prevail in the end—which you can never afford to lose—with the discipline to confront the most brutal facts of your current reality, whatever they might be."* [53]

---

[53] Jim Collins, *Good to Great,* (NY: HarperCollins, 2001) p. 85

—

One morning (as many of these stories go), I was driving on the interstate to work and it happened. Again. My insides collapsed and I lost my mind. Just like that, I wasn't myself. And I wanted more than anything to drive into a tree. I wouldn't even feel it: death on impact, and I'd have immediate relief.

Within this narrowing, strangling tunnel of my upside-down brain, I knew I could still make one choice. I had to drive in an area where there were no accessible trees and where I'd be forced to stay under sixty miles per hour. This sounds ridiculous, and it is, but my mushy soup of a brain wouldn't let me drive into a tree unless I met those demands. By degrees, I sauntered off the highway onto a local road, where trees were too thin and too inconvenient to reach, and where I couldn't drive fast enough to die instantly in a crash.

The urge slipped away. The sick twist here's that I was just depressed enough to want to drive into a tree, but too depressed to try driving into one if it was difficult to do. *Within these awful parameters, I had to choose to keep living by making it difficult to die.* Those are the sorts of choices that sound small and absurd, but in those crucial off-guard moments, they make all the difference.

"You cannot choose whether you get depressed and you cannot choose when or how you get better, but you can choose what to do with the depression, especially when you come out of it."[54]
— Andrew Solomon

—

Here are a few things to consider about what we can choose to do before, during, and after depression. *Please feel free to disagree with or to add or subtract from the following assertions.*

- Seeking therapy and medicine require intentional steps and research. They're still a choice that we must choose to make. Not everyone has the resources to secure therapy and medicine, but if you can, try them as early as possible.

- What we "digest" is especially crucial in influencing our mental state. One survey respondent said, "Upbringing and experience can really count for depressive tendencies [but] it's a choice with the kind of music, media, and reading materials you feed yourself."

- Sometimes the power of choice has to be entrusted with another person. During depression, our brains can betray us and become the enemy. We can't trust ourselves to lead ourselves even when we're sober and rational: so much more

---

[54] Andrew Solomon, *The Noonday Demon*, (NY: Scribner, 1961) p. 69

when we're depressed. Handing the reins to an understanding friend or an entire community can mean all the difference for survival. "[We have] a choice to go out and get help," one respondent said. "We're only human and our bodies can only handle so much."

- Recognize that many social factors are outside our control, and yet it is possible to get involved in changing them. Whether by petition, charities, awareness, or advocacy for your depressed friend or family member, it is possible to begin the waves of social change, and it starts by how we approach mental illness in our local communities.

- A regular routine can greatly affect how often and how much we're depressed. A respondent said, "I can't originally decide whether I'm going to start feeling depressed but I can choose whether I'm going to work out, be consistent with my medication, or assign myself to do something social every week."

Another respondent said, "I used to believe self-care and coddling were synonymous, that the best way of curing depression was to stay as far inside my comfort zone as possible. Stay in, watch my favorite movies over and over, binge on desserts, don't put any effort into anything that might 'exhaust' me. Then I realized I had already committed suicide, by refusing to *live*. Now, I get out of depression by doing new things with new people, taking risks, putting in effort on big and small things. Long story short, huddling inside a blanket eating ice cream may be comforting enough for one day, but it's not the way your whole life should be led. Raising the bar for myself is the best way I can think of to develop a life that's worth living, and not just a tolerable one."

And another said, "I believe depression is a disease. However, speaking of my own experiences, our choices do matter and affect our depression. Just like someone needing to rest more when they are sick, people with depression should seek out the activities, conversations, and relationships that give us *hope*."

> *"[About self-talk:] Have you realized that most of your unhappiness in life is due to the fact that you are listening to yourself instead of talking to yourself? Take those thoughts that come to you the moment you wake up in the morning. You have not originated them, but they start talking to you, they bring back the problems of yesterday, etc.*
>
> *"Somebody is talking. Who is talking? Your self is talking to you. Now this [Psalmist's] treatment [of Psalm 42] was this; instead of allowing this self to talk to him, he starts talking to himself. 'Why art thou cast down, O my soul?' he asks. His soul had been depressing him, crushing him. So he stands up and says: 'Self, listen for a moment, I will speak to you.'"*[55]
>
> — Dr. Martyn Lloyd-Jones

> *"I thought I could describe a* state; *make a map of sorrow. Sorrow, however, turns out to be not a state but a process."*[56]
>
> — C.S. Lewis

---

[55] Martyn Lloyd-Jones, on Psalm 42, *Spiritual Depression* (MI: Eerdmans, 1965, 2002) p. 20-21
[56] C.S. Lewis, *A Grief Observed* (NY: HarperCollins, 1961, 1996) p. 59

Chapter 5
When It Rains:
From Above and Below

Suddenly, Rain

If you've ever been punched in the face, the first time is a startling, extraordinary experience. It's almost insulting.

I still remember my first time: I was eleven and had just gotten my black belt; I was in the big kids' sparring class and up against a twelve-year-old who was six feet tall. I was beating him pretty badly and he suddenly burst into tears and punched me in the jaw. I was so surprised that I laughed. I spun around rather dramatically on one heel and I threw both my hands out, as if to stop the floor from hitting me, too. I managed to steady myself. My sparring partner had walked off, wailing. I couldn't eat hard foods for a week.

Sometimes depression is that way: a simple punch in the face with no complex reasons, no social complexities, no biological build-up—just a sudden shock to the system. Depression can occur by a **crisis event or situation** and, like a face-punch, will spin you around and leave you surprised and reeling.

But after getting hit in the face once, the next time isn't such a shock. In the same way—to stretch my cheeky illustration—knowing the kinds of crises that cause depression don't always make it easier to persevere, but an awareness of how and when it happens can keep us on guard. Such knowledge can help us brace for the impact and stop us from piling self-blame on top of the wave.

I'd also like to think of it this way. The first time we were *attracted* to someone, we felt a surge of emotions that was an overwhelming rush. In all likelihood, we reacted to it in all kinds of goofy, embarrassing ways: we were simply not ready for the onslaught of new emotions.

If we could inoculate ourselves with readiness for the next wave of depression, we might reduce the flailing even by a few degrees.

Preparation, really, is half the battle. Knowing what's coming can also remove some of the panic and anxiety. We can clear some of the debris and build a rough road-map.

This chapter will cover some common crisis situations, and suggestions on how we can manage them.

A note: Most crises events cause grief, which is a normal response. But if your grief persists for longer than two weeks (by most medical estimates) or there's complete numbness or suicidal ideation, please seek help immediately. Check the appendix in the back of this book for numbers you can call.

Manic, Panicked Genius: Are You Not Entertained?

In a candid interview in 2015, talk show host Conan O'Brien confessed that he uses antidepressants.

He explains that his depression was never about suicidal thoughts or a low self-worth, but **performance anxiety**. He would see his workplace and fall into a "fog" each day because of the enormous pressure for creative output.

The medicine, he says, was a "lever" to get the creative juice flowing, to move past the initial fear and paralysis. In fact, in a bit of a psychological pretzel, he was using his **depression as a catalyst for his creativity**, but eventually decided it wasn't worth the cost. "I used to think I needed to be incredibly unhappy to be funny," he says. "You get to a point where you'd rather be happy."[57]

A slew of celebrities have recently confessed to battling with depression, including Dwayne "the Rock" Johnson, Selena Gomez, Lady Gaga, Bruce Springsteen, Adele, and Chris Evans. It's possible that much of this has to do with the work itself. Actress Kristen Bell, best known for her lead role in *Veronica Mars* and as Elsa in *Frozen*, says, "I shatter a little bit when I think people don't like me. That's part of why I lead with kindness and I compensate by being very bubbly all

---

[57] Conan O'Brien, interviewed by Howard Stern, "Conan O'Brien: Like You've Never Heard Him Before," *The Howard Stern Show*, Sirius XM, Feb. 25, 2015 https://www.howardstern.com/news/2015/2/26/conan-obrien-like-youve-never-heard-him-before/.

the time, because it really hurts my feelings when I know I'm not liked. And I know that's not very healthy, and I fight it all the time."[58]

This sort of performance-driven depression is familiar to creative artists. The creativity creates output, which induces anxiety over the performance, which can lead to depression, which is *then* used to fuel creativity, and so the cycle continues. On top of this is the criticism, competition, and pining for "the big break" in the industry. Every step of the creative-performance process has its own pitfalls into a depressive episode.

The works of art themselves can reinforce a dark, grim view of reality, particularly when it involves tragedy or the depravity of human nature. To get to that tortured place, an artist often enters a nihilistic worldview that isn't easily shaken.

Elizabeth Gilbert, author of *Eat, Pray, Love* and *Big Magic,* warns against the fetish of **artistic misery**. She writes, "I stand firmly against German Romanticism and its obsession with creative misery and the icon of the tormented artist," she writes. "The nightmare of artistic torment is the ethic that says

---

[58] Kristen Bell. " Kristen Bell, Chris Evans and what happens when celebrities talk about anxiety and depression." Interview by Sam Jones, *Off Camera*, quoted in *The Washington Post*, May 8, 2016.
https://www.washingtonpost.com/news/arts-and-entertainment/wp/2016/05/08/kristen-bell-chris-evans-and-what-happens-when-celebrities-talk-about-anxiety-and-depression/

that our suffering shall be our badge of honor as artists, and that our genius will ultimately destroy us."[59]

The idea of depression rather than depression itself can become a codependent identity, where it's a false fuel for purpose, productivity, and meaning (more on this in the next chapter). The problem is that such a fuel is unsustainable, and as experience shows, often unnecessary for creativity.

"And the Oscar Goes to ... Not the Other Four Nominees."

On the opposite end of the spectrum, there's the pressure that a "meaningful life" can only emerge from *following your dreams*, from a sweat-and-blood passion, from succeeding not only at what pays, but what makes waves.

In other words, the post-millennial message is that leaders, pioneers, and dreamers are creating real contributions, while everyone else — mechanics, bus drivers, waiters, cashiers, to name a few — is "settling for less," or simply not sexy.

Consider the counter-argument from a subject of photo-blog "Humans of New York":

> "I work at a machine tool automation company. We build the machines that build the cars ... I started out sweeping floors

---

[59] Elizabeth Gilbert, "IT'S BETTER TO BE A TRICKSTER THAN A MARTYR." *Elizabeth Gilbert*, Jul. 7, 2014 http://www.elizabethgilbert.com/its-better-to-be-a-trickster-than-a-martyr-i-recently-did-a-radio-interview-o/

at the factory, then I got moved into the saw shop, and now I do electrical installation. I'm up to $17 an hour now ... There's actually a lot of opportunity in my field. There's not much competition. Nobody my age wants to do this stuff. They all want to go to art school or make video games or something. I think maybe it's because too many people are being told to do whatever they want. Because no matter what you think you can be, there's still gotta be people like me."[60]

This is the old dilemma of Do-What-I-Love or Do-What-Will-Pay, but with the added stress of succeeding at both. Many of those who do not achieve such "greatness" end up with an *intrapsychic pain* around the loss of what could've been, which is inches away from depression.

This hyper-expectation is completely demoralizing to blue-collar workers who are seen to have "gotten the job they settled for, not the one they wanted." It appears only wealth, fame, or groundbreaking creativity count in our millennial race towards relevance.

We're often told, "You're going to do something great with your life. Dream big. Be somebody." These are wonderful sentiments, *but we're constricted to succeed in a very suffocating range of prestige,* so that anything less than our oversized goals is considered failure.

The hyper-romance of "doing what you love," while a worthy goal, can't be the *only* goal. The employee above has

---

[60] *Humans of New York,* Interview by Brandon Stanton, Nov. 16, 2016
http://www.humansofnewyork.com/post/153264883486/

learned to "love what you do," regardless of how "sexy" it looks.[61]

In author Seth Godin's seminal work *Linchpin*, Godin makes the de-motivational case that in the post-millennial era, blue-collar *and* white-collar workers are both seen as expendable cogs. Jobs have been flattened by the assembly line of corporations and over-specialization. The doctor is now just as "plain" as the doorman. The dreamer no longer has a special pedestal over the janitor, delivery driver, or barista. This inadvertently levels the playing field. It sounds crushing, yet offers a particular liberation: *Your dreams don't have to be "big" to aspire to them.* And I don't think they ever did.

I found countless studies and surveys that showed unrealistic expectations plague every category of person, from college students to super-moms to overzealous Facebook users.[62,63,64] One of the studies called it a *quixotic hope*, named after the infamous literary figure Don Quixote, who attempted to do justice in the world and was driven mad by chivalry.

---

[61] See the principle of Job Crafting by Amy Wrzesniewski, in which her research suggests that those who see their job as a "calling" and transcend their job description are often much more satisfied in their work, no matter what kind of work it is.

[62] Katharine H. Greenaway, Margaret Frye, and Tegan Cruwys, "When Aspirations Exceed Expectations: Quixotic Hope Increases Depression among Students," *PLoS One*, Sep. 9, 2015; 10 (9). Students were negatively affected by over-expectations even five years later.

[63] Elizabeth Mendes, Lydia Saad, and Kyley McGeeney, "Stay-at-Home Moms Report More Depression, Sadness, Anger," *Gallup*, May 18, 2012

[64] Mai-Ly N. Steers, Robert E. Wickham, Linda K. Acitelli, "Seeing Everyone Else's Highlight Reels: How Facebook Usage is Linked to Depressive Symptoms," *Journal of Social and Clinical Psychology*, Oct. 2014; 33 (8): 701

The only way to avert this sort of quixotic hope is to properly invest into reasonable goals. Yet even then, we may still fail or be rejected.

Glass Ceilings and Brick Walls

Failure and **rejection** are both severe interruptions to our efforts, the former being internal and the latter being external, and they tend to inform our own self-regard.

Failure feels like hitting a wall, while rejection feels like the wall has hit you. They are crises that are a natural part of life, and even when there's no coinciding depression, they are terribly difficult to overcome.

Both failure and rejection can go hand in hand. Imagine yourself as a five-year-old handing your teacher a drawing you made, and she immediately throws it in the trash. This would feel like a failure because, "My drawing wasn't good enough." It would feel like rejection because, "My teacher dumped it with the apple cores and pencil shavings."

The thing is, **we can't help but tie our value to our efforts**. As many lectures and books have espoused, "Quit fixing your value to your results"—but there's *always* going to be a stab of pain when our sincere attempts come up short.

Opportunity necessarily involves a risk because we open ourselves to fall flat on our face, and such vulnerability opens us to condemning ourselves when we fail or when we're rejected. In turn, it can quickly lead to a spiral of depression, where we're paralyzed and cannot imagine how to try again.

When superstar MMA fighter Ronda Rousey had her very first loss in her professional career, she later remarked in an interview, "I was sitting in the corner and was like, 'What am I anymore if I'm not this?' Literally sitting there thinking about killing myself. In that exact second, I'm like, 'I'm nothing. What do I do anymore? No one gives a s___ about me anymore without this.'"[65]

Many of the comments on social media took her apart, with such statements as, "Everyone loses, get over it," or, "You can cry with your millions," or, "You're making light of 'real depression.'"

These cruel comments forget how much we're driven to equate performance with self-worth. But on top of that, it's foolish to think that wealthy, successful, athletic superstars are immune to depression—if anything, I'd assume they're more susceptible. Success is no vaccine, and any fall from such a great height can be catastrophic. It's equally frustrating to say that achieving your goals means you *can't be* depressed. In fact, sometimes a positive change, such as getting married or landing a promotion, can also be the catalyst for depression, as the pressures of these new experiences pile on anxiety and even a fear of success.

For some, the depression arising from failure and rejection is not as public or obvious. Some of the survey respondents

---

[65] TheEllenShow, "Ronda Rousey Discusses Her UFC Upset." Filmed Feb. 2016. 06:17. Posted Feb. 16, 2016 https://www.youtube.com/watch?v=iwCdv9iR8P8

wrote that it's possible to keep functioning through major setbacks while all along, depression is chipping away.

Whether these crises are public or private, negative or positive—there's a challenging, internal work that must be done around *detaching our self-worth from results and re-attaching to a celebration of the work itself, regardless of the outcome.* Or as St. Alphonsus Ligouri said, *"Those who do something for the glory of God are not troubled at all by failure, because they have already achieved their purpose of pleasing God by acting with a pure intention."* This is a lofty proposition that will never be followed perfectly—but maybe that's the point. Never perfectly is okay.

No, this internal work is still not a safeguard against depression. Yet my hope is that we may emerge on the other side with *some* of our self-worth intact, even if we barely scrape by in tattered shreds.

Minor(ity) Stigma

The pressure to "dream big" isn't merely a millennial mindset, but such pressure is prevalent in minorities and the ethnic groups from which they originate, such as my own fellow Asian-Americans. Our work ethic is mainly driven by honor and shame: success brings honor, and anything less brings shame. Naturally, this is a recipe for burn-out, disillusionment, and all sorts of neurotic mental illnesses.

The extra layer with minorities and ethnic groups is that *any depression from our failed efforts is not consoled or confessed, because of a fear that depression is "weakness."*

One of the survey respondents, an Asian-American, wrote:

> Coming from an Asian family, the general misinformation and ignorance of mental health issues can be really frustrating. I don't blame them. They were raised on values of grit and hard work, which makes it hard to understand that results aren't everything. I specifically remember something my mom said after she saw scars on my arm from self-harm: "Why are you so unhappy? We've given you everything." Shamefully, I answered that I didn't know why. We barely understand our own feelings, so asking us why really doesn't help. It only makes us more frustrated with ourselves because we don't know, either.

My guess is that the Asian-American culture, including other ethnic groups, especially pride ourselves on our heritage, strength, and overcoming adversity, but this proves to be a double-edged sword: success is set to an impossible standard, and depression is dismissed as a kind of unnatural character flaw which can be "set right" by even more hard work.

I've often heard from other Asians about depression: "We don't believe that sort of thing." The first generation of immigrants tells the second generation, "If you've been through what I've been through—" or, "You don't know what hard work is," or, "I don't have time to be depressed."

These insecurities run throughout many minorities living in the States. Sixty-three percent of African-Americans believe depression is a personal weakness, which is worse than the national average of 54% (which is still terrible), and African-Americans perceive more hostility from therapists.[66,67] Asian-Americans are likely to avoid treatment for mental health,[68] even though suicide is the eighth leading cause of death for Asian-Americans (compared to eleventh for other racial groups)[69] and Asian-American college students have higher suicidal ideations than most other races.[70] The only group with higher suicide rates are Native Americans.

There's additional anxiety to minorities in America who have historically suffered abuse under medical "care." They find it justifiably difficult to trust such institutions. With horror stories like the Tuskegee Experiment and the horrific work of J. Marion Sims, it's no surprise that minorities are nervous about anything related to the medical field. There's

[66] Earlise Ward, Jacqueline C. Wiltshire, Michelle A. Detry, Dr. R. L. Brown, "African American men and women's attitude toward mental illness, perceptions of stigma, and preferred coping behaviors." *Nursing Research*, 2013, 62(3), 185-194

[67] Madonna G. Constantine, "Racial Microaggressions Against African American Clients in Cross-Racial Counseling Relationships. *Journal of Counseling Psychology*, 2007, 54(1), 1-16

[68] Margarita Alegria, David Takeuchi, Glorisa Canino, et al., "Considering Context, Place, and Culture: The National Latino and Asian American Study," *International journal of methods in psychiatric research*. 2004;13(4):208-220

[69] Melanie Heron, "Deaths: Leading causes for 2007" *National Vital Statistics Reports*,2011; 59, 8

[70] Aileen Alfonso Duldulao, David T. Takeuchi, Seunghye Hong, "Correlates of Suicidal Behaviors Among Asian Americans," *Archives of suicide research : official journal of the International Academy for Suicide Research*, 2009;13(3):277-290

inherent suspicion of racism and the fear that minorities will be treated as subhuman by opportunistic clinicians.[71,72]

So we have a compounded issue: high work ethic can suffocate minority groups (and certainly can affect all people), there's high anxiety over the medical community because of potential prejudice, and any resulting depression from all these factors are seldom discussed.

This is certainly a crisis of culture.

In South Korea, where the suicide rate is the second-highest in the world, the tide is slowly changing *because the problem has been treated as a crisis*. The problem is rooted entirely in the cultural narrative: the elderly attempt suicide in high rates because they no longer want to be a burden on their families; high school students are in a highly competitive culture of sixteen hour days with a final CSAT (College Scholastic Ability Test) that largely determines their future; a former Korean president killed himself in 2009 after he was investigated for bribery. There are also very public suicides of Korean celebrities that lead to massive increases in suicide across the country, often copycat suicides with the same method used by the celebrity. A nationwide program for

---

[71] A study shows that black patients are half as likely to receive painkillers in the hospital, perhaps because they're considered "tougher" than white patients, which is exactly the narrative that keeps minorities from sharing with vulnerability.
Astha Singhal, Yu-Yu Tien, Renee Y. Hsia, "Racial-Ethnic Disparities in Opioid Prescriptions at Emergency Department Visits for Conditions Commonly Associated with Prescription Drug Abuse," *PLOS ONE*, Aug, 8, 2016, 11(8): e0159224

[72] There has also been noted gender bias in the diagnosis and treatment of mental health. Men and women are either treated the exact same or very differently. Women might be more likely diagnosed with depression, even if they meet the same baseline as men, and men might find it more difficult to admit a struggle with mental illness. "Gender and women's mental health," *WHO*, http://www.who.int/mental_health/prevention/genderwomen/en/

suicide prevention, including rescue crews, reduced media coverage of suicides, reduced access to harmful materials, and smartphone apps, has begun to lower the national suicide rate.[73,74]

The improvement began when the story was changed.

Entropy into Dust

Failure and rejection can also feel *final*. Sometimes, they really are. Mistakes and setbacks can't always be made right again. We don't always get back up. The closed door may stay shut. Those relationships might be gone with no way back. That brings us to the permanence of loss.

Loss is a crisis event with an *irrevocable finality*. That includes death, divorce, disease, career change, moving, broken friendships, community splits, aging, financial ruin, tarnished reputation, parting with adult children, parting with your parents, an unexpected transition, and the relentless passage of time.

All of these events create their own particular **grief**. In the excellent series *Broadchurch*, the bereaved mother of a deceased daughter explains grief:

---

[73] "On Patrol with South Korea's Suicide Rescue Team," 13:28. Posted May 2, 2016 https://www.youtube.com/watch?v=5jYBWBlEd0U
[74] "Suicide Rate," OECD (Organization for Economic Cooperation and Development), Accessed on Jun. 12, 2007 https://data.oecd.org/healthstat/suicide-rates.htm

"I used to assume that grief was something inside that you could fight and vanquish, but it's not. It's an external thing, like a shadow. You can't escape it, you just have to live with it. And it doesn't grow any smaller. You just come to accept that it's there."

Grief, our response to the vacuum-punch of loss, is a healthy reaction, and many of us will grieve appropriately (considering the awful circumstances). But there may be times when grief leads to chronic depression—compounded by a culture that despises the idea of loss.

I've found this despisal of loss most true in the hospital. Nearly every patient I visit is dealing with grief over **sickness** and **aging**. This grief is natural, but pop culture has done a terrible disservice in de-normalizing these losses. *Our modern cultural narrative is preoccupied with youth, vitality, and commodifying our appearance,* at the exclusion of anyone less than Photoshopped. Inevitably, we lose the ability to cope with those losses.

The sick and aging are seen less as an inevitable part of life, and more as grotesque, worthless, and unthinkable. With Instagram modeling and CW television shows starring a "hot young cast," the sick are unseen and the elderly are demoralized.

I hate to harp on this note, since it sounds old-fashioned to blame "these young punk kids" and "this unruly generation." Our fear of mortality has always been an understandable problem. But our view of sickness and aging has drastically morphed into a strange blend of denial and distaste, turning mortality into immorality and seeing youth as the sole currency of value.[75]

Let's consider: Social media is a relatively new platform, and we now get to watch everyone from the early 21st century aging in real-time. Those who were already "old" entered into social media with no digital memory of their younger selves, so their grief over aging has been kept in a smaller circle. Young celebrities, models, CEOs, stay-at-home moms, and fitness gurus will now have to face their mortality on a public stage.

This new dimension to aging has an **anticipatory grief** that we haven't really caught up to. It's a sort of *cultural lag,* in which we haven't learned to cope with severe leaps forward in technology, which in this case, is our instant digital catalogue of other peoples' lives. There are a handful of studies linking Facebook with depression because of "social comparison," and the article itself is called, "Seeing Everyone Else's Highlight Reels." [76] That applies to achievement as much as it does to appearances. Again, I hate to sound like a technophobe, because I truly do love our new global inter-connectedness—but the side effects are also very new, and I'd imagine it's difficult to find help for "side effects from Facebook."

---

[75] See the YouTube video "YOU LOOK DISGUSTING" by My Pale Skin
https://www.youtube.com/watch?v=WWTRwj9t-vU

[76] Mai-Ly N. Steers, Robert E. Wickham, Linda K. Acitelli, "Seeing Everyone Else's Highlight Reels: How Facebook Usage is Linked to Depressive Symptoms," *Guilford Press,* Nov. 8, 2014, http://guilfordjournals.com/doi/abs/10.1521/jscp.2014.33.8.701

I often wonder how the younger adopters of social media (including myself) will be able to *psychologically handle* aging in twenty or thirty years. Will we be embarrassed to post a newer picture of ourselves? Will we feel lost in an ever-changing youth culture? How will Instagram models and fitness gurus adapt to their platform as their appearance changes? In short, *In thirty years, will our heads literally explode in the mirror?*

According to the CDC, while the elderly are at increased risk of depression, *depression is not a normal part of aging.*[77] The majority of the elderly lead satisfied lives and have been able to cope with sickness and mortality. But this is in terms of our elderly population today. According to WHO, the global elderly population is expected to nearly double in the next thirty-five years, from 11 to 22%.[78] My own prediction is that with 1) the wide window of social media and 2) a "newer" elderly population, *depression in this group will exponentially increase.* **Our current digital age, I can only presume, will undermine how we cope with aging.**

I've found so little research and dialogue on this issue (besides grating, anti-materialistic tirades) that I'm aware I may be wrong, and many of us may age gracefully with acceptance. Maybe I'm overshooting and we will cope just fine, as most of us have before.

---

[77] "Depression is Not a Normal Part of Growing Older," Centers for Disease Control and Prevention, Mar. 5, 2015, http://www.cdc.gov/aging/mentalhealth/depression.htm
[78] "Mental Health and Older Adults," World Health Organization, Apr. 2016, http://www.who.int/mediacentre/factsheets/fs381/en/

But I predict there will be a psychological epidemic of social-media-related depression that will come from watching ourselves grow old, perpetuated by the increasing panic around aging.

Picking On Picking On Picking On —

Our digital age has also brought an entirely new dimension to bullying. From sixteen-year-old Amanda Todd to fifteen-year-old Phoebe Prince to thirteen-year-old Daniel Fitzpatrick, these teens were not only bullied online until they took their own lives, but were also mocked on social media *after* they had died.

Bullying is already difficult enough to manage in physical encounters, but the online component makes it nearly impossible to regulate. "Cyberbullying" still has little legal consequence, and parents and teachers cannot easily trace every instance of online threats.

Bullies themselves have often been abused at home and are victims of bullies themselves, with parents who have no idea that their children are bullying others.[79,80] Each category of individual—victim, perpetrator, victims-turned-perps, and

---

[79] Melissa K. Holt, Glenda Kaufman Kantor, David Finkelhor, "Parent/Child Concordance about Bullying Involvement and Family Characteristics Related to Bullying and Peer Victimization," *Journal of School Violence*, Vol. 8, Iss. 1, pp. 42-63 Jan. 2, 2009

[80] Melissa K. Holt, David Finkelhor, and Glenda Kaufman Kantor, "Hidden Forms of Victimization in Elementary Students Involved in Bullying," *School Psychology Review*, 2007, Vol. 36, No. 3, pp. 345-360

the parents who neglect or abuse them—can suffer depression, as both the cause and effect of these roles. And bullying is not merely an issue in grade school, but a much more subtle force in workplaces, politics, and the economy, where aggressive tactics are hidden with polite smiles and legal loopholes, and the victims must learn to play nice in fear of losing their positions.

Further education and prevention programs have had limited success and, truthfully, the more I read on the topic, the more I felt both angry and helpless about the ugly, unbreakable cycle of bully to victim to bully. My only hope really is that children and adults can have **transparent conversations** and a constant, open venue to speak. Early dialogue can offer coping mechanisms and quick accountability. I say this knowing even such openness is no guarantee to save a life, but it *is* guaranteed that nothing will change if the hurt is hidden and hushed.

PTSD over PTSD

Another consequence of our digital access is a front seat to **violent news** and national grief, and just as harmful, the ugly dialogue and demonization that accompanies every tragedy.

Perhaps the most ironic element here's that violent crimes on a global level have gone down to its lowest numbers in history, but the news coverage and its accessibility have only gone up.[81]

More coverage can be good because awareness can lead to action. But more coverage can also set in a deep cynicism about humanity. We can become continually numb to tragedy and fall into the familiar hopelessness of depression.

On top of this, the tragic cycle of outrage, grief, and vitriol on social media has been "normalized." But the human brain isn't meant to handle so many violent headlines; some suggest it's caused a national outbreak of PTSD and anxiety.[82]

My guess is that not only does the tragedy itself cause depression, but the media carnival surrounding it also causes a kind of feedback loop, a sort of PTSD over the PTSD, and we're still catching up on how to mourn at this level.

That brings us to a less obvious problem with our emotional capacity. After a tragedy, we're quicker to react on social media, sometimes for unsavory reasons—getting views, "likes," and followers—which skips a very crucial step in the grief process. In fact, social media seems to skip the entire process itself. When we short-circuit and bypass our grief, it's dangerous: no one has the capacity to bottle up so much trauma.[83] That's how depression can enter through the

---

[81] It's true that year by year, violent crime fluctuates and has increased in some years. But historically, throughout the scope of human existence, the average death toll from crime has dwindled. I still do not find this very comforting. See *Sapiens* by Yuval Noah Harari.

[82] A study by Pam Ramsden in 2015 surveyed 189 participants who had viewed violent news on social media and rated their clinical level of PTSD, finding a significant correlation. However, the study has not yet been peer reviewed.

[83] Various studies have shown that suppressed emotions, including grief, can lead to harming your health. Likewise, obsessive emotions can do the same.

backdoor, because of *an unaddressed build-up of grief that bubbles up down the road.*

In the last few weeks of writing this book, there have been multiple bombings, stabbings, and shootings; some were personal, some acts of terrorism, and some are still under speculation by armchair detectives. Within hours, even minutes of these events, there were think-pieces and commentaries by pundits who offered (or imposed) their hot take, followed by thousands of anonymous comments that no child (or adult) should ever be allowed to read.

I'm wondering how many of these pundits and commenters are going to melt down. Some might need a melt-down in their process, but I'm sure that many of them will collapse involuntarily because they haven't learned to mourn in silence. They (and I) have been ringside spectators, not always willingly, absorbed in constant chatter instead of truly processing the horror of what has happened.

It's easy to be self-righteous about this sort of thing and to blame the vulture-like voyeurism of the media. But I must admit: I'm prone to the very same impulse to smear commentaries over tragedy. I often forget to slow down and remember that the news is talking about *very real lives.* I forget to hold space for grief and for mourning.

When I get depressed about another tragic headline, I'd like to think my body is purposefully shutting down to make space for the victims of violence and for their families. Our bodies crash because we crave the rest that we're not getting.

It might be a stretch to say our bodies involuntarily shut down. Or perhaps science shows otherwise. That brings us to the possible *evolutionary adaptation* of depression.

Some (Dar)Win, and Some Lose

Evolutionary scientists have formulated several reasons why we get depressed. The evolutionary hypothesis is that depression acts as an *adaptive function* for a crisis, even when we're consciously unaware of the actual crisis. The following reasons at least partially outline some of the adaptive tactics of depression and why it might be hard-coded in our genes.

1) To know when to quit.

A study suggests that the onset of depression in a new endeavor *can allow you to quit reaching for an unattainable goal.* When two groups attempted to solve an impossible anagram, the group less likely to be depressed was also more likely to keep trying the impossible. In other words, those who struggle with depression also quit earlier and saved themselves some hassle.[84]

2) To stay indoors and to shut down.

Seasonal Affective Disorder (SAD) is a type of depression that follows the seasons. It was also probably an effective way

---

[84] Katharina Koppe and Klaus Rothermund, "Let it go: Depression facilitates disengagement from unattainable goals," *Journal of Behavior Therapy and Experimental Psychiatry*, February 2017, Vol. 54, pp. 278-284

of coping with winter when winter was fatal; it kept you indoors away from life-threatening exposure. Depression can be a way of your body hibernating, for a kind of *waking sleep* to recharge for the next season. It could've also helped prevent the use of excess energy in a stressful situation.[85]

3) For realistic insight and assessment.

The phenomenon *depressive realism* tells us that the depressed have a better handle on reality.

The advantages have been empirically measured. Those who struggle with depression can accurately gauge how much time has passed and how productive they were.[86] They're less risk averse in financial investments.[87] They also measure themselves with a bit more humility, which is the very opposite of the Dunning-Kruger effect, in which someone has an unrealistically high view of themselves (think of every angry *American Idol* contestant who really thought they could carry a tune).

There are multiple Reddit threads which lift up depressive realism as simply a *realistic view of life itself,* and that depression is a "perfectly healthy reaction" to a bad situation.[88]

---

[85] One major problem with this theory is that many communities had to work even harder during the winter to survive, and evolution would assume that only hard-working people would be left after a disastrous winter.

[86] Diana E. Kornbrot, Rachel M. Msetfi, Melvyn J. Grimwood, "Time Perception and Depressive Realism: Judgment Type, Psychophysical Functions and Bias." *PLoS ONE*, 2013; 8 (8): e71585 http://journals.plos.org/plosone/article?id=10.1371/journal.pone.0071585

[87] Lisa A. Kramer and J. Mark Weber, "This is Your Portfolio on Winter: Seasonal Affective Disorder and Risk Aversion in Financial Decision Making," *Social Psychological and Personality Science*, Jul. 18, 2011, Vol. 3, Iss. 2, pp. 193 - 199

[88] "Depressive realism is the proposition that people with depression have a more accurate perception of reality," *Reddit*, Jan. 20, 2010,

However, "depressive realism" has a debilitating disadvantage: it entails a view of life that is pessimistic, fatalistic, and absurd. It's to see the world through Edvard Munch's *The Scream*, with no reprieve. There's a continual self-deprecation and a current of existential resignation, as if life were all a stream of floodwater rushing into the sewer. So "depressive realism" can run so far the other way that it once again becomes a liar.

4) To demand a change.

A growing hypothesis is that depression is the body's way of demanding a change, much like a work crew goes on strike until the employer meets the crew's conditions. A hunger strike is the same, except it says, "I'm ransoming my own health until you change." Depression might be a mixture of both, bargaining the health of the depressed person so that others can rush in.[89]

It's possible that postpartum depression is the mother's body saying, "I don't have enough resources to do this on my own; my body is shutting down so you have to help." Since early humans raised a child by the entire community's involvement, perhaps mothers are still wired by the mantra, "It takes a village."[90]

---

https://www.reddit.com/r/science/comments/arspv/depressive_realism_is_the_proposition_that_people/
[89] Edward Hagen, "The Bargaining Model of Depression," *Genetic and Cultural Evolution of Cooperation* (MA and England: MIT Press and Dahlem University Press, 2003) pp. 95-123
[90] I want to be careful here and note that the "postpartum bargain" is only a *hypothesis* and certainly only one explanation out of many.

The advantage here's that even though the depressed person might not consciously ask for help, the body waves a flag as an honest signal to others. Both the depressed person and the community would need to respond to the depression.

These evolutionary explanations to depression seem to be both a gift and a curse. They're a gift because they protect the body from crisis, but they're a curse because they cause an involuntary shutdown of your brain. It's like an unwanted kill-switch that self-destructs the entire vessel.

While I'm not entirely sold on the evolutionary hypothesis, I can also see the potential benefits. At the same time, I'm not sure I would *ever* tell a depressed person in their moment of crisis that their body is "just adapting."

And in the end, *sometimes there's no reason at all.*

Aliens from Inner-Space

An episode of depression can truly strike from out of nowhere. Whether it's caused by broken biology, social breakdown, or early trauma, it's all the same result: the brain can seemingly erupt into a depression with no external provocation, becoming its own crisis event.

Up to now, we've been looking at **exogenous** depression, which occurs from the outside-in, like taking punches in a ring. Then there's **endogenous** depression, which occurs from the inside-out, as if from a volcanic eruption.[91]

Again, most forms of depression are exogenous, meaning that we can trace many depressive episodes to a specific, external cause or event. But about a quarter to one-third of those with depressive episodes are afflicted for endogenous (internal) reasons.

While I've had many episodes of situational depression, I've suffered largely from the abrupt trapdoor of endogenous depression.

The scary, horrible thing about endogenous depression is that an episode can hit you at any time, for no reason, from zero to freight train in a second.

Endogenous depression can strike in the "healthiest" of people, who don't have a history of mental illness, by zero fault of their own. *In these cases, there's a biochemical cause that's physiologically wired in a dormant, embryonic form, that can erupt without an inciting incident and is often uncontrollable and irrational.*

An endogenous episode can fall like rain without warning. It's sporadic, with an acute onset, quicker than a thunderclap. Like a grenade, the pin is pulled, and we're forced to work triage on an injury in the battlefield.

A study from Harvard Health shows that at least 30% of suicide attempts are impulsive, with only minutes between

---

[91] These definitions of are simplified and require further exploration than I can do here.

the thought and attempt,[92] and the New England Journal of Medicine states at least nine out of ten people who attempt suicide never try it again.[93,94]

The uncertainty of this lightning-bolt depression also sets me on a severe psychological edge, always waiting for the next stomach punch—and the anxiety has become so suffocating that *I've fallen into depression over the fear of being hit by depression.* It's maddening, and yes, ridiculous.

"Thanks, I Feel Worse."

Maybe learning about some of these crisis events only increased your anxiety rather than preparing you for the next one.

So basically everything causes depression? Thanks, I feel worse.

This can be good news and bad news.

The bad news is that, yes, a ton of things cause depression. The good news is that, no, there's no such thing as a "pointless reason" to get depressed.

I think I've beaten myself up when I felt a crisis was "too small" to worry about, much less get depressed over. I would

---

[92] Annmarie Dadoly, "Suicide is forever, but the stress leading up to it is often temporary," *Harvard Health Publications*, Mar. 21, 2011, http://www.health.harvard.edu/blog/suicide-is-forever-but-the-stress-leading-up-to-it-is-often-temporary-201103211957

[93] Matthew Miller, "Guns and suicide in the United States," *The New England Journal of Medicine*, Sep. 4, 2008, http://www.nejm.org/doi/full/10.1056/NEJMp0805923

[94] Suicidality and depression can be two different issues. Those who attempted suicide were not always depressed beforehand, and those who are depressed are not always at risk for suicide, since depression can remove the motivation for action entirely.

hand-wave a lot of my issues as first world sensitivities. I'd often tell myself, "You don't know what suffering really is." I'd think my credit card debt was incomparable to a starving child in Somalia.[95] And I still think so.

But events like failure, rejection, aging, and loss are universal across generations and cultures—and pain is pain. A debt is not the same as starvation, but neither event cancels each other out, and each experience contains its own challenges. There are *always* larger problems across the globe, but comparing the two does nothing to address either one.

All that to say: Your depression is *yours*. No one can say your crisis is too small for your emotional fallout. While this doesn't mean we should wallow in self-pity, it also means that we don't have to justify our reactions.

Your process is yours.

Your grief is yours.

Your depression, as hard as it is, is owned by you and you alone. No one can make a claim to it—and to have even a small shred of such ownership is power.

---

[95] This is a logical fallacy called The Fallacy of Relative Privation, or "the appeal to worse problems." *Your issue X is nothing compared to all the poverty and genocide in country Y.*

Chapter 6
Reality Versus Romanticism:
Everyone's In On It

Disclaimer: This may be a difficult chapter for those who suffer from depression, but I plead with you to stick through to the end as I attempt to balance every angle of the discussion.

Stealing Thunder

One of the stigmas around mental illness is that it often sounds like an excuse. The difference is that everyone wants a good excuse—but sufferers of mental illness aren't looking to suffer. We would "snap out of it" if we could.

As much as I'd like it to be true, depression isn't a cover; it isn't "antisocial" or "moody" or "flaky." It's a completely debilitating fog that suffocates rational thinking. When I'm sad, it's manageable. When I'm depressed, it's downright intolerable. There's nothing about it that I want to flaunt or fake.

Unfortunately, **the word "depression" has been increasingly hijacked into a cult-like subculture of quirkiness,** so that it *does* sound like an excuse. "Depression" and its cousins anxiety, bipolar disorder, and introversion are used flippantly as a lifestyle, a cheap dress for trending bloggers, a kind of non-conformist calling-card to appear relatable, and yes, even a retroactive excuse for laziness.

This is an extremely difficult matter to approach, and even now, I feel sick at the thought of casting more doubt and fear on the suffering who want to find help. I don't ever want to say there's a "right way to be depressed" or that we have free rein to judge who has "real depression." I absolutely want to believe every story of mental illness, at face value, without equivocation.

But I also don't want the word "depression" to be so easily thrown around that we are in fear of being laughed down. Such nominal piggybacking of real issues always cheapens the actual issues and the people within them.

If any other illness, such as cancer or heart disease or Alzheimer's, was faked for decoration, the outrage would be swift and merciless, and rightly so. If I'm to treat mental illness as seriously as cancer, I cannot shy away from this very tricky balancing act of making space for the depressed while calling out the fraudulent few. It pains me to say it, but this casual masquerade of faux mental illness *does* happen.

My hope is that you'd stick with me to the end of this chapter, as I carefully attempt to be fair to every side of this discussion and reveal the larger truth behind our motives, which may surprise you.

I'll Have What She's Having

Why would anyone even fake an illness as awful as depression?

I believe that a certain **romanticism of mental illness** has seeped its way into our global culture, from Hollywood to music to social media, portraying mental illness as quirky, desirable, and attractive. With a couple of flourishes, mental illness can be framed as a glamorous, triumphant battle, or a haunting, artistic foray into nihilistic pondering. But anyone suffering from such an illness will tell you: there's nothing desirable or attractive about dealing with a broken brain each day. And to capitalize on that is diminishing and insulting.

I say this with clenched teeth: *My suffering and yours has often been minimized into a secondary, self-pitying prop for profit and attention.* Our suffering has been assembly-lined for mass consumption. Like with any other market: everyone wants a piece.

Many of the surveys I conducted were bitter about the hijacking of depression as a marketable brand. One respondent wrote, "Some people think depression is black and white photos on your Instagram and staying home for the day." A respondent went as far as to say she was sick of the word *stigma*. She wrote, "I am tired of the talk about stigma—we get it by now. The word depression is being diluted, I think it's just become a saturated market honestly, which really discounts the intensity of my experience ... Depression and other mental illnesses [have become] a kind of 'fun label' for people to toss around and use as a defense for shady behavior."

Another respondent spoke at length about a subculture of *fashionable death and depression,* in which the self-labeled "depressive" would blast anyone who "didn't understand me," would compete over how much medication they were taking, or post pictures of self-harm as bragging rights. The respondent, regarding this "trend," says:

> "I almost felt guilty if I wasn't 'depressed enough' or if I didn't go as far as others with self-harm ... I do believe they are genuinely depressed, but I wish they would recognize that fact as a need to get help rather than encouraging others to come down to their level. Honestly, I hate writing that, but it's the truth."

One of the first recorded instances of fashionable depression can be seen in the 1620s-30s of England, only a few decades after Shakespeare's *Hamlet* entertained the masses with mental illness. It was called *melancholia,* a blanket term that perhaps captured actual depression, but also covered moodiness, "mopishness," and other emotions that were self-diagnosed as "abnormal." Historian Michael MacDonald writes, "Melancholy and gentility became boon companions. Noblemen delighted to have themselves painted in the guise of melancholy lovers ... an ordinary country fellow was too stupid to be melancholy." It was "an affliction of the privileged."[96]

Clark Lawlor, professor of English Literature and author of *From Melancholia to Prozac: A History of Depression*, also makes the case that melancholia was a persona of mad brilliance used for "social advancement" across sixteenth-century Europe. He writes:

> "The melancholy 'malcontent,' a usually disaffected young man frustrated in his progress up the slippery ladder of ambition, became a recognised social type by about 1590. The individual in question would have at least a self-image of talent, if not genius, but also a perception that the world, for reasons of its own, was refusing to recognise that Saturnine blessing of great ability."[97]

Fast-forward to today, and a cursory search online shows article titles like, "Depression: The New Black?", "Ten Reasons Why It's Fun to Suffer from Depression," and, "Don't you just love my new, trendy illness?" Quora and Reddit threads about depression are littered with angry comments about teens trying to be "quirky and weird" with mental illness, and one comment stating, "Anybody that thinks depression is something cool ... has never experienced how deep it can go and how crippling it can be." Bill Oddie, English TV personal-

---

[96] Michael MacDonald, *Mystical Bedlam: Madness, Anxiety, and Healing in Seventeenth-Century England* (NY: Cambridge University Press, 1981) p. 149, 151

[97] Clark Lawlor, *From Melancholia to Prozac: A History of Depression,* (NY: Oxford University Press Inc., 2012) p. 62

ity, harps against celebrities "coming out" as depressed: "I don't think that the life of a celebrity can be compared to, or relatable to, a normal, everyday life, so I don't know how much good it really does."[98]

This glamorization happens in more subtle ways in our echo-fest of social media, where death or disorders are exploited for publicity. Comedian Michael Drucker, in the excellent podcast *The Hilarious World of Depression*, talks about riding the coattails of someone else's suicide:

> "I can't commit suicide because I'm just worried that all my friends might write three paragraphs about themselves on Facebook. Whenever you know someone who commits suicide, it's like everyone writes this long post about *their* personal relationship with this person ... I can't kill myself because someone's going to get two hundred 'likes' off my death. That's a funny way to convey it, but there's also a real existential fear that someone else will use my death for attention."[99]

"White Man's Sickness"

None of this is okay. Hijacking mental illness has severe, disruptive consequences across the world.

---

[98] Richard Eden, "Celebrities are making mental illness fashionable." *The Telegraph*, Nov. 10th, 2013 http://www.telegraph.co.uk/news/celebritynews/10438044/Bill-Oddie-Celebrities-are-making-mental-illness-fashionable.html

[99] John Moe interviewing Michael Drucker, "6: Supershow! Eight Comedians! One Chronic Mental Illness!" *The Hilarious World of Depression.* American Public Media. Podcast audio, Jan. 16, 2017

I received an email from a native Nigerian, who wrote that the general perspective of his country towards depression was that it was a first-world problem. He writes,

> "A lot of us [Nigerians] never thought depression was something that would affect people around here. Nigerians mostly saw depression as 'white man's sickness.' We've seen depression as an excuse by westerners to be lazy and unproductive. Many Nigerians wonder how being constantly sad can be a disease."

He goes on to say that millions of Nigerians are silently suffering from depression, but feel afraid to tell anyone because they'll be accused of latching onto a westernized, glorified vanity.[100]

My guess is that there are many other reasons why someone would hide their depression (which we explored in previous chapters), regardless of ethnicity or culture, and it's unfair to use dismissive phrases like "white man's sickness." But the problem remains: *when someone hijacks a real illness for style, then those who are actually sick will lose their voice.* The hurting will silently suffer, afraid to look like a self-serving faker.

This subculture of faking harms also harms those who want to help. Consider that there's now a serious art of "busting the faker." From food allergies to service dogs to

---

[100] He writes, "Just search on Google, lots of results there," which I did, and found statistics of up to 48 million Nigerian sufferers of depression, which is about 14% of those who suffer worldwide.

military veterans, the pretenders are getting their just exposure.[101] Unfortunately, every time a faker is discredited, suspicion is cast on every side: the public begins to wonder if the problem is a real problem. This suspicion then blends the truly suffering with fan-club bandwagoners, and no one knows the difference.

I don't believe that "faking depression" is the norm, but as with any sort of movement on awareness, a small fringe group can steal the thunder and become an out-of-control cyst. When a subculture becomes the loudest voice on a serious issue, it waters down the voices who are hurting.

—

So here's where we are.

I believe that the over-saturation of "crying wolf" about depression has led to a **backlash**, a sort of reactionary tug-of-war between three groups: 1) "trendy depressives," 2) outsiders, and 3) the truly suffering.

Outsiders, stuck in the middle, can find it difficult to know who is truly suffering. **The real sufferers then are afraid to speak up, not because talking about it is a stigma, but because talking about it feels so passé.**

It's very possible that, just as the concerned man from Nigeria implied, the western romanticism of depression directly contributes to our fear of finding help.

---

[101] Sophia Harris, "People with serious food allergies want impostors to stop faking it in restaurants," *CBC News*, May 28, 2017

This leaves the depressed person in a double-bind: *silence is self-destructive, but talking about it is seen as proselytizing for the cult of attention.*

This causes sufferers to hide even further.

How, then, can we tactfully approach the subculture, the spectator, and the truly suffering?

A Cry for Help, a Lie for Help

Despite all my critique, I have two optimistic theories on the romanticization of depression, both which hope for a good end.

I have to say again: I can't call out who is "faking," and I never would. I'll go one further: *I believe those who are hijacking mental illnesses as a trend are certainly in need of their own recovery.* Those who go so far to seek attention this way need both our empathy and an honest confrontation. And maybe it's not so much that anyone is "faking," but that there's a much deeper heartache underneath the posing.

There's a reason why people cry wolf and why we want to be heard, even under false pretenses. **A lie for help is still in some ways a cry for help.** Thunder-stealing is its very own dysfunction, and it requires its own process of healing.

I've found that those who thunder-steal the word "depression" are likely covering for something else. In fact, *those who use "depression" as a label could still be truly depressed themselves.*

Yes, "emo kids" and the like can genuinely be suffering from any number of issues, so it might be a chicken-and-egg situation. To set *true sufferers* against "fakers" can be a false dichotomy, and I'm certain there's an overlap. Our motives are not so black-and-white, which is all the more reason we must explore them.

Stealing thunder, really, points to a need we all have, depressed or not: *a need for validation, to be heard, to be received.* Many of us can fake our way through a social bubble to gain that acceptance. The same goes for those with mental illnesses: any one of us can self-diagnose and work our way into a group that will listen. If that sounds like a crude accusation, my guess is that most "fakers" are not even consciously aware that they're faking. They may have superficially checked off a few symptoms of mental illness *in order to find a welcoming community.* So if anything, that's more of a condemnation of our neighbor's increasingly closed doors. It's not on the person who is trying to break in.

I'm reminded of *Fight Club,* in which the lead character becomes addicted to therapy groups for the terminally ill: it's a horrifying subplot, but it resonates with painful, biting truth. We can easily switch tribes and latch onto labels in search of what C.S. Lewis calls *the Inner-Ring*: the place where we finally, fully belong.

As it turns out, the groups for those with mental illnesses are generally a welcoming refuge. It's a testament to people with depression that we would be so quick to welcome others. We don't want to question a person who claims they're depressed; after all, that's exactly what the world already does to them. We receive anyone at face value *exactly* because we've been shut down and cut off for so long. So it's understandable that the doors would be busting open: the "world of the depressed," by its very design, is much more compassionate than most other communities.

The downside is that a few fakers might get in. Or rather, a few self-convinced, self-diagnosed people looking to belong somewhere would be attracted to a community of lovely, open survivors. How could I blame them?

Even the truly suffering can squeeze their own communities for over-validation. I admit that I'm tempted to seek a little glory and pity from my condition sometimes. **We're all equally capable of crying wolf**, and it doesn't require an entire subculture to enable us.

I can very quickly mine my own depression to deflect responsibilities, just like little Peggy Ann McKay who "cannot go to school today." I've used my own legitimate depression as a get-out-of-jail-free card. It's appalling, but it's also human nature. As much as I hate to admit it, I'm not so high and mighty that I'm above that sort of thing. Can you, fellow fighter, admit that this happens, too? Because the faster we can confess it, the better we can fight the actual wolf.

—

Here's my second theory on the romanticization of depression. Consider first an excerpt of a literature review from *The Journal of Mental Health*, which coins the term *extreme communities:*

> "A number of 'extreme communities' have formed online, such as pro-anorexia, pro-suicide, pro-amputation and likely-psychotic groups. These serve to provide support, outside a medical and social mainstream that finds their beliefs and behaviours unacceptable."[102]

In other words, **when a stigma of silence surrounds an issue or person for too long, the only kind of community left for that issue or person will be an extreme community.**

They appear dialed to eleven, but it's because they've had to fight to be heard. They had to shout. I'm not endorsing *extremism,* but rather, lamenting that someone would have to shout to be heard at all.

In the case of depression, these extreme communities are more likely expressing joy, pride, and relief that they've found one another, as if they've "come out." And as these communities become more mainstream, they will include the uglier sides of human nature: the competition, the gratuitous self-promotion, and making a fetish of their own cause. *These subcultures will inevitably romanticize and glorify themselves.* It's part of the human package.

---

[102] Bell Vaughn, "Online information, extreme communities and internet therapy: is the Internet good for our mental health?" *Journal of Mental Health.* Aug. 2007; 16(4): 445 – 457

The previous article suggests these extreme communities are both a risk and a benefit. On one hand, these groups can reinforce harmful behaviors and increase self-harm. They can enable faking for the wrong kinds of attention. On the other hand, these groups can help "normalize" what sufferers are going through so that they don't remain alone. They can enable maladaptation, but can also become a real source of empathy.

I remain cautious of "extreme communities," but *for many of the truly suffering, our best option might be to join an extreme community until we are more embraced by the mainstream.* Sometimes joining an extreme community is *exactly* for the purpose of being heard by the mainstream.[103]

I'm imagining how a hiding sufferer must be overjoyed to find a place where other sufferers are rewarded for honesty and for freely expressing themselves, even if it seems gaudy and over-the-top.

My hope, eventually, is that depression could be seen as seriously as cancer, alcoholism, or autism, so that we will not be clawing so hard for a platform. I'm hoping that the stark line between extreme and the mainstream can dissolve, or at least become permeable. For now, I empathize with extreme communities, because despite their less savory antics and the possibility of posers, they might be someone's very last bastion.

---

[103] There are layers to this. Sometimes a personality type such as introvert can become pathologized, which leads to associating the "undesirable traits" of introversion with depression. It is easy to see why extreme communities can be so attractive.

Breaking Up: My Love Affair with My Love of Depression

We need a bit of a gut-check here.

On one hand, no one should *ever* be afraid to confess their depression. There's no "right scale" for this sort of thing, and for those of you who are teetering on the brink of depression, whether from moodiness, discouragement, or stress: you still need grace and an open space to receive empathy and a listening ear. The last thing I want is to instill any more fear or second-guessing. If you feel that you need help, no one (including me) must stop you.

On the other hand, if I sound aggressive towards the romanticism of mental illness, it's because I'm unequivocally, unabashedly angry that anyone would knowingly or unknowingly use such labels to service their own egos.

I can't imagine that every single "self-diagnosed" blogger who posts a litany of sad songs, rain GIFs, and angry poems must be consciously faking. But I also strongly believe that there must be some self-deception.

I've raised the counter-point that there are legitimate reasons we romanticize mental illness: 1) our inherent need for validation, and 2) an unhealthy lack of real community. Yet it's these two needs, whether by cause or effect, which have inadvertently perpetuated the recruitment of bandwagoners who have no interest in mental illness except for self-interest. That is where I must draw the line.

The following is a gut-check-list that might clarify where the *romanticized subculture of pseudo-depression* has muddied the waters. It is *not* necessarily to determine if your depression is "fake" (though that's worth exploring), but to determine how much you've bought into the romanticism of mental illness and made it a prop.

By clearing up our motives, we can find healthier expressions of depression that are not aimless self-promotion, and perhaps find help for issues that we never knew existed.

I hope we're willing to confront ourselves (not each other, but ourselves) with these dreaded but much-needed truths.

Please believe me when I say that I write the following list with reluctance and hesitation, but I write it in the hope that some of us who will dare to examine what's inside.

- There are some who claim to suffer from depression but have not been clinically diagnosed or are greatly exaggerating such claims. Depression doesn't need a diagnosis to be real (and in many cases, resources are lacking for both a diagnosis and a treatment), but has there been an actual diagnosis by a certified professional? How is the word "depression" being used?

- Some who claim to suffer from depression or suicidal ideation may have immersed themselves in "dramatized" literature or music or social media, and such bombardment cultivates a kind of intermittent emotionalism. I believe *this is not the same as depression*. Have you found yourself attempting to incite such a mood?

These emotional cues are manipulated, as opposed to the unwanted visitor of depression. Watching a "tearjerker" or listening to a "sad song" or having a "dark blog" only provoke a temporary state, similar to forcing yourself to cry. Occasionally, such pensive moods, when reached in healthy ways, are even necessary to grow and mature. And if entertainment constantly causes uncontrollable weeping or other involuntary symptoms, this may actually be a sign of depression or something else.

- Self-pity is not depression. If depression is a fog-state in which we are collapsing inwards, then self-pity is generally the opposite, a pathological kind of "fishing for compliments" and unhealthy victimization that expands outwards and squeezes people as if they're receptacles of validation. Do you find that you are self-victimizing, akin to stretching out a cold or flu longer than the illness actually lasts?

- Depression can certainly be a part of your identity, but there's a point when (the idea of) depression is elevated to *be* your identity. How much internal exploration has been done to differentiate between identity and over-identifying?

- I'm a big fan of gloomy art and cynical prose and dark satire, but there's a point when such expression becomes a self-promoting carnival, which only parodies the truly suffering. Any kind of media that is glorifying or fantasizing about death and mental illness is especially belittling towards the suffering. What does your media intake look like? What does your media output look like?

- Phrases like "I'm depressed" or "I want to kill myself" or "I'm suicidal" are not meant for casual use. If you use them, why? And when?

- If you suspect that you're both participating in a subculture *and* legitimately suffering from depression, I'd kindly like to ask, "How is the subculture helpful? How has it constructively added to the conversation around mental illness? How do you feel about unsubscribing from certain blogs or deleting your own? Are any of your motives from self-promotion? Is there a better way?"

- Do you feel "excitement" or a "high" from telling others about your mood? Why?

- Do you feel inordinately angry when someone asks questions about your depression? Do you feel immediately "oppressed" or "persecuted" whenever the topic of depression comes up? Do you presume that when someone doesn't understand you, this makes the person immoral or "bad"? Do you feel more patient or impatient when you explain your depression to someone?

- Have you ever appreciated when someone listened to your story, even if they didn't respond the way you would have wanted? How specific are you about the way you want your depression to be "respected"? How likely are you to dismiss someone if they don't respond to your depression the way you would have wanted?

- If any of the previous suggestions have bothered you, I'd kindly like to ask, "Why? What bothers you about it? What kind of rights do you feel like are being taken away? What are the objections and why do they come up? Are those objections a position that is worth fighting for? Even at the expense of possibly contributing to a mockery of depression and your own?"

Part 3
The Hero's Quest

*Choosing a Sword,
Slaying the Dragon, and
Surviving the Way Back Home*

*A journey to find light
in the dark of depression.*

Chapter 7
"Solutions"

A Psycho-Analysis
of Psychoanalysis

When I began to look into therapy, I was overwhelmed by the buffet of options. Gestalt method or Freudian analysis? Skinner's behaviorism or Rogers' humanism? Secular or religious? Conventional, or music and chanting a mantra?

Since therapy sessions average about one-hundred dollars per hour without insurance: I had some anxiety. A lot of anxiety.

On the podcast *Invisibilia*, from an episode called "The Secret History of Thoughts," hosts Alix Spiegel and Lulu Miller trace a chronological line through three forms of therapy.[104]

1) Traditional Psychotherapy: *Your thoughts come from something deep within you.*

Discovering a connection to your current issues by exploring trauma, childhood, and formative events. Examining your "true motivations," to understand why you do what you do, may be the goal to mastering and managing the associated

---

[104] Lulu Miller and Alix Spiegel, "The Secret History of Thoughts," *Invisibilia*. National Public Radio. Podcast audio, Jan. 9, 2015

emotions and behaviors. This method was founded by the infamous Sigmund Freud, who also established defense mechanisms, sexual fixations, and all the weird Oedipus stuff.

2) Cognitive Behavioral Therapy: *Your thoughts can be managed with better thoughts.*

Replacing patterns of thinking and behavior with alternative patterns. There are different forms of CBT, but the general idea is to re-frame how we see the world by changing the lens. You learn to differentiate what is actually happening from your idea of what is happening, and those altered cognitions can ward off false destructive thoughts.

3) Mindfulness: *Your thoughts are not you, and can be released.*

Being mindful and aware of what's happening inside, and allowing harmful thoughts to "float away" by disengaging from them. It might be similar to, for example, watching a movie and suddenly being aware it's "just a movie," and then the emotional spell of the film is broken. An offshoot of CBT, mindfulness incorporates some Eastern philosophy, including the use of meditation and controlled breathing.[105]

The podcast seems to imply that each new therapy is better than the last, so that "traditional psychotherapy" has been

---

[105] As a general rule, according to professor Mark Williams and Danny Penman, Ph.D., more "active" people do well with CBT and not medicine, and vice versa with "passive" people.

outdated and overridden. That might not have been the intention of the hosts, but I was troubled by the idea that therapy kept changing.

The other problem is that every therapist has their own baggage, biases, and personalities. Your friend might recommend a therapist that worked for them, but he or she absolutely does not work for you—not because the therapist was bad, but because he or she did not fit your needs.

That's the main problem with "solutions" for mental illness: it appears there are an infinite number of variations on getting help, *and it seems you might not ever find the right one.*

I've Tried It All and It's All Been Done

Just as some therapies are better than others, what works for many will not work for all—and what works will keep changing.

The first research I did for this book was to look up other books on depression. For every positive review on a book's Amazon listing, there was a scathing review that declared the flaws and contradictions of the author. The author's "solutions" were exposed as Swiss cheese. These plot holes seemed rather big and unsettling. Why hadn't the author addressed these in the editing stage?

Some choice quotes from negative reviews:

"Eh."

"Totally ridiculous concept. Apparently the way to avoid depression is to just not think."

"[The author's] advice is to think happy thoughts ... Its offerings are so shallow and contraindicated, it is on the border of malpractice."

"[This book] uses a one size fits all approach to explain depression. I don't need my depression explained. I need to find comfort in a book, not facts and examples."

"According to [the author] we are responsible for our depression and must basically pull ourselves up by our boot straps in order to get out. Just sucking it up and toughing things out is what I have been doing all my life and this book was not supportive or encouraging."

"The book is pure garbage. Don't waste your money. I don't believe the author is a PhD. A kindergarten kid could do better. No scientific value at all."

"The author has an obvious slant for using medication as a quick solution. Supporting the pharmaceutical industry for a lifetime and giving up sex is not what I call healing."

"[The author's] henchmen have belittled my review and tried to get me to take it down. All it did was remind me of how adamant I feel that this book is snake oil."

"You would do well to read a few of the negative reviews, they have a lot of important things to say about why this book is not as great as popular opinion seems to think."

I quickly learned that no matter how comprehensive, articulate, or scientific the book was, *it was never going to be enough for every person who suffers from depression.*

There's certainly good advice we can heed and bad advice we must avoid, but there appears to be no singular template that can successfully address it all.

Even worse, it seems on a long enough timeline, we become immune to even the best forms of treatment. Depression is a slippery, slick demon that changes from person to person as much as it changes individually within us.

The Swiss cheese "plot holes," most of the time, were the many differences between the readers and authors.

I started to find this all very bad news.

The Good News: The News Is Not New

Here's a liberating truth. It's a direct implication of the bad news.

Since no one particular method exists for "curing depression," this means *you don't have to beat yourself up when it doesn't work.* Methods fall short because that's all they are:

methods. When they fall short, it doesn't mean *you* have. The blame for this isn't on you.

I've angrily wondered if I'm not trying hard enough, not pulling up those boot straps, not doing exactly as the doctor ordered. Some of us get our hands on a new kind of therapy or medicine, which all but guarantees our recovery, and when it doesn't work, our depression worsens.

I was convinced for a time that I must be "the only guy" who couldn't be cured. All these success stories about making it to the proverbial *light at the end of the tunnel* would only crush me. Of course, I was absolutely happy for those who were recovering by a new method. I couldn't diminish that. But I still felt stranded outside the winner's circle, beaten down by inspirational testimonies, suspicious of superlative claims.

It was a shock when I learned that *there's no winner's circle.* No one "wins" at depression. **Recovery is a multi-faceted strategy of trench warfare that doesn't hinge on a Holy Grail, but a holistic process.** At the end of each day, even the "winners" are limping, bloody and ragged, to the finish line, with a joy born from tears and tired hands.

The whole thing can seem like a lifelong feud, an ugly street fight that requires a diverse arsenal, with ready reflexes to switch out the tools whenever necessary.

And there will always be new methods. Many of these new techniques deliver for a time, and even for a long time. Yet I'm now prepared when any book, counselor, or therapy begins to show cracks and weaknesses. I feel the freedom, even duty, to throw out the book or change my therapist. And I know that none of these by themselves will be wholly complete.

That may not be news to you, and it may not even sound like a good thing—but it was absolutely liberating for me.

I could quit blaming myself if some method failed to work. I could quit thinking something was so horribly wrong with me that I was beyond hope. I could quit the desperate race to find the next-best-thing that would "finally work this time."

Comedian and actress Maria Bamford, who has Type-II Bipolar disorder, found only medication worked. She says:

> "I do feel better, and it is all the result of drugs. I have done [every] kind of emotional sudoku you can do. Like if it's been put in a book, or cognitive behavioral therapy, or twelve step program—I have worked the program. [I did] therapy groups, and I am a consummate exerciser, all that stuff. I've been touched by healing hands, with light, while ceramic angels surrounded me in a strip mall. I've done everything, and meds topped them all. Do everything that you can to get some good help, but know that it's hard. I've had everything available to me, and it's [still] hard."[106]

She swore by medicine. By process of elimination, she found what worked for her. By such tenacity, slowly and painfully, I believe so can we.

---

[106] John Moe interviewing Maria Bamford, "2: Maria Bamford Talks Bipolar II While Her Pugs Eat Nilla Wafers," *The Hilarious World of Depression.* American Public Media. Podcast audio, Dec. 19, 2017.

Solutions (Sort of)

In addition to medicine, therapy, and support groups, I'd like to advocate for one more solution—sort of. [107]

In an episode of the podcast *The Hilarious World of Depression*, the host John Moe talks about the therapy of bizarre, unorthodox hobbies. He's careful not to offer it as a "cure" or a substitute for treatment, but rather, as an individual alternative for each person, according to how we're each wired. Moe interviews a depression survivor who has learned the ukelele and another who has taken up penguin spotting, both who find their hobbies relaxing and mindlessly enjoyable. [108] There's a paradoxical element of both routine and spontaneity that seems to dull the gravity of depression.

The thing is, a placebo is still helping. Anything that can take your mind off the pull of depression, for even a second, is still working. (Anything that's reasonably legal and innocuous, that is.) And those placebos, those little mental placeholders, are usually weird and unexpected.

I have a strangely secretive "zone-out" hobby that's my break and buffer: I love reading about movies. I love reading about cinematography techniques, line reading choices, the director's reasoning behind a particular shot, the subtle flicks of an actor's face that tell purposeful stories. I don't plan to do

---

[107] There's a list of other therapies in the Appendix of this book, including hotlines.
[108] John Moe, "PLACEBO: Therapeutic Ukuleles, Therapeutic Penguins, Therapeutic Yarn," *The Hilarious World of Depression*. American Public Media. Podcast audio, Apr. 24, 2017

anything with the film industry. I just eat up the nuances of film.

There's nothing really in it for me, except that it's for *me*.

I think many of us are convinced that productivity is the only way to be, and there's a guilt when we're not "using our time wisely." But our brains really do need a moment to get lost in *the essence of something in itself, an activity done for its own pleasure, for the beauty of what it is.* That's not just about fighting depression, and it's not just a placebo, but about finding a pure joy without agenda, about soaking in the essential glory without it paying off in some tangible way.

I don't think these "motive-less activities" suddenly whisk away depression. But I know that for me, when I'm in the routine of them, I'm less likely to get depressed, and I can recharge for what's next.

Hope Is Not a Postcard, But a Battleground

In a pivotal scene in the show *House,* the titular character Dr. House is in a therapy session with Dr. Nolan.[109] House has just been released from an institution and he tries cooking to overcome his addiction to pills.

---

[109] *House.* Created by David Shore, episode written by Sara Hess and Liz Friedman. FOX and NBC/Universal. Original air date: Sep. 28, 2009

House: My leg's killing me. Cooking helped for a while. I guess I got bored. My leg started hurting again, then I got worried, and that made the pain worse.

Dr. Nolan: What are you worried about?

House: That nothing's gonna help. That I end up in the very dark place. I'm fine, just not happy.

Dr. Nolan: I didn't let you out because you were happy. I let you out, because I believe you had the skills to cope with that. You tried one thing. It didn't work. So move on. Write. Play chess.

House: What if nothing works? What if nothing gives me more than a few days before my brain starts looking for the next fix? Before my leg feels like someone's shoving nails into it? What do I do then?

Dr. Nolan: If nothing in the world can hold your interest, we'll deal with that when we get to it. But you have to trust me, and you have to be patient.

If you feel like you've tried everything and none of it's working: I'm with you. I'm as cynical as it gets.

My hope is that you'd have hope.

That you'd expect something will fit you.

That even reducing *some* of the symptoms, for *one more day,* is considered a win.

The problem with a methodical solution is that it can't account for the mess inside. I've been duped into thinking that I can plug into an equation, and when the math didn't add up, I ended up crumpling myself into the waste basket.

Maybe it's because we were set up for failure. In a culture of Three-Point Outlines and Seven Super Habits and Perfect Pragmatic Plans, we were misled to demand a cut-and-dry, copy-paste diagram. Maybe we can free each other of that postcard hologram, and simply expect the gritty, unromantic, slobbery journey of fighting for our very lives.

I believe, despite many false starts on many failed methods, that there's hope for recovery. It's possible. I also believe it's a battle to get there, and that "getting there" will look different from the pretty picture in our heads.

I've been at the height of frustration, when I was trying what everyone else recommended, and it wasn't enough. But I've learned that even an exhausted victory at the end, with pieces of my sanity still intact, was good enough. That two or three methods at once, remixed to my own disposition, was just fine. That even when a method didn't "fix me," it was never meant to: but only a way to push through one more step in the dark.

I had to learn to celebrate those tiny steps.

I've learned not to be let down if my recovery didn't hold up. There was always another way.

Glory Yet Possible

I want to tell you about "Jen," who offered to share her story. Not every story ends this way, but Jen gave me hope that sometimes *we can truly, completely win.* With the help of Jen's therapist, she was able to communicate her heartrending struggle and eventual victory.

Jen grew up with a very physically and verbally abusive mother. Jen's mother always told her that she was a rape baby, wasn't wanted, and wasn't loved. After mercilessly beating Jen, her mother forced her to look her in the eyes and say she loved her, despite what Jen was actually feeling. The beatings were frequent, at home and in public, and Jen felt she was constantly walking on eggshells, doing all she could to avoid upsetting her mother.

Jen's father was an alcoholic and drug addict; he left the home when Jen was a baby. Jen's stepfather and two of her cousin's husbands sexually abused her. By the time Jen was sixteen, her mother left, and Jen went to live with a distant religious family, furthering her shame and disconnection. She learned from an early age how to build walls, keep people out, and protect herself from being hurt.

As an adult, Jen dated a married man for years, and she soon had a non-viable pregnancy, furthering her guilt and shame. Jen continued to be in a relationship with this man, believing the narrative she had learned in childhood: she was unlovable, worthless, inadequate, dirty, didn't matter, and deserved nothing better.

When Jen went to therapy, she had recently broken up with the married man, and she was having chronic nightmares, flashbacks, crying spells, panic attacks, no support, low self-esteem, and was severely depressed. Jen also admitted to having a negative attitude, partially because of the way she was raised. Jen teetered between sobs, explaining that she felt like she was a lost cause and would never get better.

But if you were to meet Jen today, you would never recognize the woman previously described. Jen spent over a year in therapy, sometimes twice a week, fighting for her recovery. Despite the many tears and deep pain it brought up, Jen continued to show up to therapy, week after week. Jen processed her trauma with EMDR, an evidence-based trauma treatment model, and in time Jen began to transition from being a victim to a survivor to a thriving person.

Jen is now in a healthy committed relationship, and is looking towards marriage. Jen attends a church, and is not afraid to reach out for help and support. She no longer suffers from PTSD or depression. She finds herself thinking about happy memories, positive thoughts, and is able to live life in the present. Jen no longer ruminates and obsesses over her past. She no longer believes the lies she was told in childhood, and has come to recognize the strong and resilient person she is.

While therapy can't change what has happened, it did rewire Jen's brain so that her memories no longer continue to affect her in the way that they used to. For Jen, looking back is like looking at a picture, without any sting of sadness or anxiety.

Having done therapy will not exempt Jen from experiencing future pain, but having processed all of her trauma, it is likely that Jen will continue to reach for support and know that she is worthy of care and connection. Jen is able to manage life without feeling overwhelmed by it, acknowledging that life is painful and messy, though worth the courage to share and connect with authenticity and vulnerability.

Chapter 8
Everyone Leaves

Disclaimer: This is yet another difficult chapter for those who suffer from depression. It contains very unpopular opinions. We may disagree, but my hope is that this chapter raises discussion about the limits and boundaries of how we can help.

Idealistically / Realistically

After an episode of depression—

—sometimes your friend will leave.

It's not okay that they do, but it happens. Depression is no friend to friendship. It takes us hostage and has us saying and doing things we normally never would, and even though *it's not really us*, the hurt we cause is very real.

This is an incredibly unpopular opinion because it seems to advocate more for those who deal with the depressed over the depressed themselves. Of course, I'm on the side of the depressed (and oppressed and victimized and persecuted), and they are my number one priority.

Idealistically, we would all lean into the wounded and stay with them, with not a single thought of abandonment.

But *realistically*? People leave.

While I once considered the ones who left as heartless and cruel, I'm learning to sympathize with their decisions. I don't blame them: my depression is so severe, I cannot imagine enduring with someone like myself.

Dealing with a depressed person like me is exhausting and draining, and it requires much more help than many of us can give. Those who stayed with me had a capacity for grace far beyond any human measure, including my own.

It doesn't mean that those who left are inherently bad people or have "sold out." It only means that human patience is limited, and not every temperament is designed to bear with such an overwhelming condition. Some have a longer wick than others. Some are more wired to be patient with very specific wounds and worries, and it takes a special kind of person to persevere this way.

Again, it's not okay that your friend leaves: but I want to prepare you for when they slip out the backdoor. I want you to know it'll be a harsh, angry moment of betrayal. And I had to learn to release my grip on bitterness, recognizing that we're not all saints who can pay the cost of compassion.

—

This discussion has two competing viewpoints, and I offer two quotes here to show both sides.

Consider the words of Andrew Solomon, who suffered a depression so severe that he tried to contract HIV from male prostitutes to kill himself:

"Depression is hard on friends. You make what by the standards of the world are unreasonable demands on them, and often they don't have the resilience or the flexibility or the knowledge or the inclination to cope. If you're lucky some people will surprise you with their adaptability. You communicate what you can and hope. Slowly, I've learned to take people for who they are. Some friends can process a severe depression right up front, and some can't. Most people don't like one another's unhappiness very much."[110]

Then consider the words of Stephen Fry, who told his story of bipolar disorder and depression in *The Secret Life of the Manic Depressive*:

"Try to understand the blackness, lethargy, hopelessness, and loneliness [the depressed are] going through. Be there for them when they come through the other side. It's hard to be a friend to someone who's depressed, but it is one of the kindest, noblest and best things you will ever do."[111]

On one hand, to "always be there for someone" is not some cute, whimsical montage of high-fives and breakthroughs. Movies and TV shows can make mental illness look quirky and appealing, but in real life, it's usually intolerable and

---

[110] Andrew Solomon, *The Noonday Demon*, (NY: Scribner, 1961) p. 69
[111] After an incalculable amount of searching, I've been unable to track down the source of this quote; I only found a ton of Pinterest wallpapers with the quote and no citation. It most likely comes from an interview.

insufferable. It's a grueling journey to stay with the very worst of your friend—and no one tells you about the awful smells and sounds of a person who is truly suffering.

Really, I would worry more for a friend who is overly confident in dealing with my mental illness. I worry more for friends who think they're just as capable as a therapist or a social worker. I am tired of those who throw on a cape and try to play hero-savior with all their tried and true remedies. All of my friends, and I mean *all of them,* are outside their depth to handle me during an episode. At a certain point, only trained professionals are qualified to speak into my mental illness—and even then, would they stay if they weren't trained and paid?

Some people who are depressed never hurt a single person. But some, like me, have a depression that isn't typical: it's accompanied by intense anger, violent outbursts, and days of catatonic lifelessness. It drains my loved ones and can be dangerous to myself and others. At times I'm convinced I can never love or be loved, and I end up saying painful things like, "I'm not sure if I ever loved you" or, "I'd rather die than let you know who I really am." I become both helplessly numb and deadly sincere; I say things I don't mean and that mean too much. So I can understand why some of my friends would draw tighter boundaries with me. I get why some would even choose to leave for a time.

But on the other hand, please hear what I'm *not* saying.

I'm not saying that a friend should leave at the first sign of difficulty.

I'm not saying your friend should not hear you out or stop trying.

I'm not saying that when a friend leaves, they did it for a legitimate reason.

I'm not saying that you should stop reaching out to your friend who's hurting. This isn't an easy out.

I'm definitely not saying that those who have mental illnesses are incapable of deep, lasting friendships.

I'm not "victim-blaming" or shaming those who are barely surviving.

And when it comes to your spouse and your children, unless there's abuse involved, it's never okay if a family member flakes out and leaves.

But I am saying that *it's contradictory to ask for selfless empathy for my issues while at the same time I disregard empathy for the other person who must deal with me.*

You can't have it both ways. You can't ask for empathy that you're not willing to reciprocate. And I'm afraid that because of our unrealistic, over-romanticized culture, our idea of love has become, "Put up with everything no matter what, or else you don't *really* love me"—which is atrocious, mercenary, and reeks of luxurious privilege.

Responsibility / Reaching Out

I've gotten this wrong before.

Let me tell you about Roland.

I met Roland in my third and final year of seminary. I was taking satellite courses in Florida, but for my final year, I went to North Carolina to the main campus for a month-long crash course. At the seminary gym, Roland introduced himself to me.

He was tall, a bit desperate, with shifty eye contact, the sort of good-looking guy who probably wasn't so handsome in grade school. He sort of followed me around the gym, offering to spot me, copying some of my exercises.

We exchanged shallow pleasantries between sets, and at the end, he said, "Maybe we can, uh, like have coffee this week."

"Sure," I said, unsure if I wanted to offer my number. I take longer to make friends. Trust issues, I suppose.

"Do you, uh—"

"I'll see you at the gym tomorrow?" I said. "Then we'll make plans?"

Roland grinned, a really sheepish, aw-shucks sort of grin. "Yeah, yeah!" he said, practically clapping. "Okay!"

I didn't see Roland the rest of the week, and the crash course ended. I went back home to Florida and forgot I had ever met him.

A few months later, one of the professors on the Florida satellite campus made an announcement at the start of class:

"A student named Roland committed suicide this week."

Roland's girlfriend had broken up with him. The break-up had happened months ago. *Months ago.* And he was too lonely to go on. He had swallowed a bottle of pills and went into a coma. His parents decided to withdraw life support.

I remembered Roland's puppy-dog shout: "Yeah, yeah, okay!"

I understood why he had tailed me at the gym. Why he was so quick to find a friend. Why he wanted to meet for coffee.

After class, I ran to a restroom and threw up everything inside of me.

I could've ... I should've ... I didn't.

I let someone die.

For years, I felt responsible for Roland's death. I've blamed myself over and over, seconds before my head would hit the pillow, remembering his dark-encircled eyes, replaying his voice on mental vinyl, losing sleep and softer dreams.

Could I have done something?

Should I have done something?

Every time someone talked about "reaching out" and "little acts of kindness" and "you never know who you'll help," I'd want to throw up again. The regret ate me up.

I've tried, since then, to learn the difference between *reaching out* and *being responsible*.

I've tried to learn the fine line between doing all I can and knowing that *all-I-can* is not always enough.

I should've reached out before it was too late—but I'm not sure I was responsible for what happened. Maybe I write that to absolve my own guilt, or maybe there was really nothing I could've done anyway.

It is such a precarious balance, to feel a responsibility for the safety of those who are depressed, while also maintaining a balanced boundary for your own self-care.

I've seen dozens of patients in the hospital who have tried to attempt suicide, and some who succeeded. I've read that those who want to take their own lives, contrary to popular opinion, talk about suicide very openly. When I look through these patients' charts and histories, I look for signs, red flags, some key words they mentioned to a psychologist or social worker or another chaplain that indicated they were at the end of their rope. Sometimes the signs are obvious, *but so many times, they're not.* I've wondered how the medical staff feel. *How did I miss it? Was there something I could've said differently? Weren't they getting better?*

On my social media, I've gotten dozens and dozens of messages from strangers who threaten to kill themselves if I don't reply. And when I do reply, I usually don't hear back.

I don't know how to be a ransom to someone's suicide. I'm not sure where the line is between seeking attention and really needing help.

Maybe I could've saved Roland.

Or maybe it was never up to me.

I only know that if I could go back, I would have had coffee with him. I would like to have tried. I am not ultimately responsible—but I still want to reach out when I can.

I'm sorry, Roland. I'll try to hear you next time.

A Dance of Mashed Toes

I don't know how to do this.

To be friends with the depressed person is a bit of a dance with mashed toes. No one quite knows what they're doing, and we need more rest than the others, but we are trying.

My wife knows when she needs a break from me. My friends know how much they can give before tagging someone else into the ring. But really, they're trying. I'm trying. With mashed up toes, we dance this crazy dance.

My hope is that every side of this conversation can learn to navigate with each other, with both shrewdness and gentleness. Friendship, with or without mental illness, is full of messy complexity, and we will never, ever get it perfectly the first time, the second time, or the tenth. We can only try our best each time.

I also cannot demand that all my friends stay unless I empathize with the cost of their love for me. I cannot demand forgiveness without considering the deep hurt that's been caused, regardless of whether I was out of my mind.

Thank God, there are some people who stayed despite it all, and I am thankful and humbled that they would love at such high expense.

And really, if a friend leaves too early: I must question if that person was truly a friend at all, or only liked the parts of me that were palatable. In that case, they will probably always jump from island to island of half-commitment and convenience, and I say, good riddance: we're better off.

I'm Here

So how can we reach out to a friend who's depressed? Another survey question I asked was:

How do you help a friend who's going through depression?

These responses were wonderful suggestions that I never knew I wanted for myself until I read them. I share them with you not as a way to "save" your friend, but to be one. And it reminds me there are many, many people who are willing to go out of their way to stay.

> Speaking for me, when I'm depressed, just treat me normally by taking me out for a meal or movie to take my mind off things.

To be humble and apologetic instead of defensive if it turns out that I'm the reason they're depressed.

More than dialogue—create a free, hospitable place through their warm meals, music, stories about other things, care packages. That means a lot and also shows the depressed person that they are not too "scary" to do life with. Warm meals and movies and music can move mountains.

Knowing that their depression isn't the same as mine, and that what works for me won't necessarily work for them. Praying with them if they want. Going with them to therapy if they want.

Randomly texting them that you're thinking about them, or randomly encourage them from time to time. Some forget who they really are, when joys, hopes, and ambitions are swallowed up by depression, I want to remind them of who they are.

When I had depression, nothing was more helpful for me than when my mom or a friend would come over and pitch in to help me clean, even if it was just doing the dishes or vacuuming the carpet. Talking through emotions is great but there's almost always something physical or substantial that can be done that lightens the load and makes everything else easier to handle.

Showing up unexpectedly to check in. Referring people to a therapist. Recognizing my limitations. Validating their feelings. Normalizing it. Sharing my own experience. Tell them they're loved. Listen to them.

I realize that my friend in depression might not be able to ask for help, so I find ways to step up when needed. If that is going to the grocery store with them, or driving them to an appointment, or just calling when I know they are struggling—having a support system is crucial.

When I got depressed, it meant the world when my friend showed up at my house and did my dishes, sat down at my computer, and looked up therapists to help me get into therapy.

Watch movies in silence. Go for a walk, a swim. Visit puppies at the Humane Society. For me, in a depression, one of my favorite things was my friend would show up and we'd lay in the grass, looking at the clouds even though tears wouldn't stop flowing from my eyes.

And my favorite:

Offering my friend to do stuff together, but respecting when they just want to be a potato is good.

Chapter 9
Without You, I Survived

I Tried to Find You

Towards the end, when she comes home later and later and stops picking up my calls, I'd get in my beat-up Corolla and actually try to find her. Windows open, stomach twisting, the December air pouring in: I have to find her.

What would I do, though, if I did?

Storm in and madly declare my love? Fight the other guy? Rant and sob and flail as they stare?

Why? Is he better than me? Do you love him?

How exactly does this scene end?

I don't know. I just want to see her.

I drive everywhere. Hotels, movie theaters, restaurants, subdivisions, complexes. I ball up my fists and strike my own forehead, *stay awake, stay alert,* mad somehow that I only have two eyes, mad at myself for doing this.

Streetlamps and billboards get mushy, the lanes shift and sway, my fingers scream. I tell myself one more building, then one more after that. I usually quit after a couple hours—but this night, I keep pushing. Concentric circles outward, twenty streets, twenty-five, scanning, I have to find—

—and there it is.

The drab olive Civic with the Columbus State sticker.

I park. Not too close, not too far. It's about three in the

morning. I breathe cold vapor, my organs pumping slime.

I knew. All along I knew.

I wait. Time distends, rolls over, escapes the car and floods back in, a heavy, feeble hand around my neck.

I wait. I sleep. I wake. The sun rises, a yellow smear of mud, caked across unmoving trees. Doors open and close, cars leave for work; I wait.

It is afternoon, and I'm so tired; the weariness has grown roots in my veins, and I wonder if this is even her car. I hear blood in waves between my temples, a tug of war tearing between sanity and obsession.

A door opens, and I think it's her. It has to be her. She's wearing an oversized t-shirt, probably his, the same shirt she's been coming home in for weeks now — *is it her? the same shirt?* — and I realize she might see me, so I pull my seat back, and for a second I think she might have seen me and panic shoots up my mouth, and someone walks behind her, a man, and I think they're holding hands, but maybe I've been sitting here too long, and I choke on winter.

They kiss. Not deeply, and not softly, either.

I turn on the car and get the hell out of there.

I cry loudly, these loud obnoxious sobs, like laughing backwards, and I'm so tired. I'm so tired. I jump into bed, and minutes later, she enters. She lies next to me. She holds me like she knows, like I know nothing.

Later that night—I haven't slept now in nearly forty hours—I rip through her closet. She's out again.

I find it. Her diary. Really, it finds me. Her composition notebook falls out from between two purses on the highest rack, a neat *plop* on the carpet, and it opens to the very page I was looking for.

I am torn, she's written. *He makes me laugh, but he doesn't understand me. The other understands me, but doesn't make me laugh. Who do I choose? My body is at home with Chris and—*

I shut the notebook, stuff it between the two purses, and I look for pills. Any pills.

A jumbo bottle of acetaminophen. I sit on the cold tile of the bathroom floor with the pills and begin to chew them. Every few pills, I call her. Her phone rings and rings, and by now I've memorized her voicemail greeting.

I call. *Six pills.* I call her again. *Nine pills.* I don't leave a message. *Twelve pills.* I end up calling her twenty-six times. About forty or fifty pills.

At nine in the morning, she finds me on the bathroom floor. I'm awake somehow. I've been awake almost fifty hours. I don't know how long I've been dead.

I tell her, *Now you can watch me die.* And I ask her, *Why did you ruin us?*

She says, *We were already ruined.*

She suddenly falls over me and grabs my shirt and says she's sorry. A hundred times, she's sorry.

I close my eyes and I smile. I am a smiling skeleton. This is what I want. I don't care what she's done. This is what I want.

This sickness in me—it is consuming.

Another whisper in me asks:
Is this what I really want?

Collapsible

It's embarrassing to remember this story.

When I tell others I've tried to kill myself in college, most assume it was because of an irreversibly traumatic loss. When they hear it was *over a girl,* there's a sort of backing away, with uncomfortable glances at the floor. I know the look: *I would never let it get that far.*

I never thought so, either. It's hard to imagine getting there—unless you're the one there.

I learned the hard way that *it's possible to get so attached to someone that you want to die.* It's possible to be so codependent that when someone leaves, you can't imagine going on. You can become sick enough in your stomach over another person that your very life is coiled with theirs. And to plant a soul in something so collapsible leads to a life that is untenable.

There's a *codependency* so overwhelming that you wait for the other person's every text, flinch at their every move, hang on their every word, cater to their every whim. It is a pan-icked, mindless, gut-squeezing desperation, a constant seasick cramp that will not let you function unless you get the look, the nod, their attention.

I know. It sounds pathetic, and it is.

On the surface, it probably looked like I really loved The Girl from Columbus State. We fell fast, and made plans to marry, and moved in together. But my over-attachment made me controlling, manipulative, selfish, neurotic, overbearing— and really, I drove her away. It was as much her decision as it was mine. I blame her, but I blame myself, too.

Even when I was with her, my bowels were filled with a throbbing, deafening dread. I was constantly afraid of losing her affections, that I was boring her, that I wasn't funny enough, charming enough, smart enough, *enough* enough. In every silence, I thought she would find me out and know I was a fake, an impostor: *It's over, I made a mistake, you're not who I thought you were.*

Her smile filled me. Her eyes filled me. I breathed her in. She was my drug. Our arguments were shrill, poisonous, thrilling, intoxicating. As long as we argued, I rationalized that she was still with me. Attention was attention. At work, at class, I devised ways to keep her entertained, these lavish schemes of hot air balloons and nights in Paris and me on a stage, performing and her clapping, me finally revealing I was a worthy catch. I was her puppy dog, until we argued again, and I was throwing things at walls until she said she would stay. She'd say sorry, and I told her I loved her, when I hardly knew what love was, I hardly knew who she was, I hardly knew who *I* was.

By the time I had swallowed half a bottle of pills, I was already dead: I was simply discarding the hollowed out husk of the person I used to be.

I never thought it would happen to me. I used to look at the codependent and think, *Break-ups happen. Heartbreak happens. People leave. You'll be okay.* Even as someone who wrestled with depression, I never understood those over-the-top, disproportionate reactions, all that silly, frivolous, first-world drama between couples.

But there's something dangerously different about the over-attached, the codependent, the *people-pleasers*, like me. It isn't just a phase. To please someone is life; to lose them is death.

Some of us, because of past abandonment or rejection or abuse, get easily addicted and attached to people.[112,113] It's not that we become attached to every person we meet—but we find those one or two people, place them on a pedestal, and turn them into vicarious mirrors for our self-worth. They fill the empty place that was once carved out of us. They're an organ transplant.

I'm not explaining it away, as if that makes it okay. But it becomes a trained reflex to use someone as a fix. It's an addiction, and yes, it is also a terrible, unwise choice.

There was a time when I'd be driving and had the radio on, and I'd change the station if I sensed the passenger wasn't into the song. I'd modify my speech patterns to fit the current

[112] Julie A. Fuller and Rebecca M. Warner, "Family Stressors as Predictors of Codependency," *Genetic, Social, and General Psychology Monographs*, Feb. 2000, 126 (1), pp. 5-22

[113] Kathryn M. Bell and Lorrin Higgins, "Childhood Emotional Maltreatment and Later Intimate Relationships: Themes from the Empirical Literature," *Journal of Aggression Maltreatment & Trauma*, Feb. 2010, Vol. 19(2), pp. 224-242

crowd around me. I'd spend hours on culture sites to know the latest catchphrase, the hottest meme, the most obscure references. My friends would love that I never complained, but really, I never voiced my opinion on much of anything, unless I was absolutely certain that I could disagree without putting the friendship at risk.

But in the end, people left anyway, long after I had pleased them. In fact, my desperation to be "that guy" probably undermined our friendships the whole time.

I look back on my old journals when I was with The Columbus State Girl, and it's all crazy, obsessed, practically psychotic ramblings of future fantasies and infatuation—and barely any of it was about her. I had never breathed her in. She only exposed what I was actually breathing: *the golden trophy world of* **me.**

I made us about saving myself.

Codependency, in the end, I think, isn't about serving the other person, but about doing good to feel good and getting good back. There's nothing wrong with feeling good or getting good, unless those are the ultimate all-encompassing motives—and then we will throw ourselves down at the mercy of such unstable waves.

The relationship—my golden trophy—was a failure before she even got there. To have made it about me, to be attached to an *idea*, was how I ended up sprawled on the cold tile with my stomach swimming in acid.

I know that my story of suicide cannot compare to those with even greater losses. I know it was a tragic error of my own judgment to allow myself to be so consumed. I don't expect pity or sympathy.

But I've learned not to scoff at those who are so easily attached. I get why it happens: *they are trying to be whole where there's no wholeness.* And I'm learning to manage my own weakness for approval, that when I feel myself stretched to another, I recognize it is a reflex, a routine that was beaten into me by the pain of a past I did not write. I am learning how to get close without becoming consumed.

I can go right back around to me and say,

I'm on to you.

I know what you're up to.

And painfully, I must sever the umbilical cord between you and my self-worth.

> "Codependency isn't sexy. It isn't romantic. It's built with a fuse and will surely burn out. The healthiest thing you can say to the one you love is, 'I would be okay without you, and that's why I choose to stay.'"[114]
> — Lauren Britt

Who Am I Without You?

In the movie *Runaway Bride*,[115] Maggie Carpenter, played by Julia Roberts, keeps running away from the altar every

---

114 Lauren Britt, Feb. 8, 2014, http://yesdarlingido.tumblr.com/post/93614942540/
115 *Runaway Bride.* Written by Josann McGibbon and Sara Parriott. Paramount. Jul. 30, 1999

time she's about to be married. A curious reporter, Ike Graham, played by Richard Gere (who else?) begins to write a story on Maggie, and he interviews all her ex-fiancés.

Ike asks the same question of each men: "Do you know what kind of eggs she liked?"

Each of the ex-fiancés has a different answer.

"Poached, same as me," one says. "Scrambled," says another. "Fried," says one more.

It turns out that Maggie simply copied each of her fiancés. Each of them assumed Maggie enjoyed what they enjoyed, when really, Maggie was only pleasing their tastes.

Ike confronts her, and Maggie defends herself: "That is called changing your mind."

Ike retorts, "No. *That's called not having a mind of your own.*"

There's a scene shortly after where Maggie tries every method of egg to discover what she likes best.

The movie, while silly and sort of a summer throwaway, has stuck with me because of this profound little arc.

Do you know what kind of eggs you like?

I had to learn what eggs I liked *for myself.*

That meant risking the horrible reality that *people might not like me,* and that if they didn't, they were just people, too, with their own worlds, lives, thoughts, and insecurities.

I can't say my stomach still doesn't get sick over pleasing people. I still get depressed about it sometimes.

But I'm trying to hold my ground, on my terms, knowing that I can't win them all—and if I win them while losing myself, who wins in that deal?

I had to discover that it was never about winning them, anyway. I had to love them more, and need them less. And *I can only love others when I enter into their lives with a surplus, and not to steal their worth for my own.* That requires knowing who I am, **to know what I'm really about**.

I had to ask myself:

Who am I without you?

What are my non-negotiables?

What am I called to contribute?

What am I made to do? To be?

What am I about?

I know that *finding myself* and *grounding my identity* are not guaranteed strategies against the darkness.

But if I could carry *what I'm really about,* a mere scrap of such a whisper, to see it, cradle it, sit on it, fall on it, fail on it, hide in it, rest in it—then I could stay with it through the dark, with a frail fragment of purpose to take another breath, and another after that one, for the possibility of another world, another dream, when one chapter has closed, and I am yet in the next one, a survivor who learned that some things are not meant to be held, but I am still there, holding.

After a While[116]

After a while you learn the subtle difference
Between holding a hand and chaining a soul,
And you learn that love doesn't mean leaning
And company doesn't mean security.
And you begin to learn that kisses aren't contracts
And presents aren't promises,
And you begin to accept your defeats
With your head up and your eyes open
With the grace of a woman, not the grief of a child,
And you learn to build all your roads on today
Because tomorrow's ground is too uncertain for plans
And futures have a way of falling down in mid-flight.
After a while you learn
That even sunshine burns if you get too much.
So you plant your garden and decorate your own soul,
Instead of waiting for someone to bring you flowers.
And you learn that you really can endure...
That you really are strong
And you really do have worth...
And you learn and learn...
With every good-bye you learn.

---

[116] Some have credited this poem to Veronica Shoffstall, an American poet, Jorge Luis Borges, an Argentine poet, or Judith Evans, an amateur poet who claims she wrote the poem before it was plagiarized. It also showed up in an Ann Landers column. In any case, the poem has been an immense blessing to me, as I hope it is for you.

Chapter 10
Healers Need Healers:
An Interview with a Depressed Doctor

I had the wonderful opportunity to interview a fellow blogger who happens to be a physician. She's wrestled with depression and helps her patients wrestle with theirs, too. She has quite the following on her Tumblr blog *wayfaringmd*, which is filled with humorous anecdotes and strong commentary about the medical field. I've been a regular reader of her blog, and it's my honor to present an edited transcript of our interview.

Disclaimer: Doctor W. wanted to inform the reader that she is not a psychiatrist, but a family doctor. The following also contains some graphic content.

J: What is your own personal experience with depression?

Dr W: I didn't really realize or admit I was depressed until honestly a month and a half ago. In hindsight now, back in college I can say I had an episode where I was severely depressed, and my friends all basically knew it because I disappeared off the face of the earth and I stayed in my dorm room in the dark all the time and skipped class. Strangely enough, my grades improved because all I did was study.

My friends were like, "You really need to come hang out because we miss you and we don't know where you are." I got to this point where I was angry all the time about anything and everything and couldn't figure out *why*, and just had this profound sadness I couldn't explain. It didn't seem to be about anything in particular. There was no big event that made me sad. It just happened. I remember being in my dorm room one weekend and all my roommates were gone and I was just lying on the floor, weeping. For me that was a big deal, because I do *not* cry, like ever. Sad movies, babies, death: nothing makes me cry.

So I was just bawling. That nasty, ugly, snot-coming-out-everywhere kind of cry. I was praying, "Somebody's got to help me, I got to tell somebody. If things keep going on like this, bad things are going to happen." I started having this thought of ... not wanting to kill myself, but, "Maybe things would be easier if I didn't wake up in the morning."

I asked God, "Give me a name of a friend who I can reach out to. Give me the name of someone who's *safe*." And a name came to me of a girl who was just an acquaintance. We weren't really super close. But I called her right then, while I was boo-hooing, she asked, "Are you okay?" I said, "I'm really not." I asked her if she could come over and talk with me for a little bit.

She came over and I told her what was going on. I think part of what had triggered my depression was that I had made really good friends the year before, and two of them transferred schools. As it turned out, my friend who came over had gone through a lot of the same things the year before, too.

For me, the most therapeutic thing was somebody else saying, "Me, too." Like this is something that happens to regular people. She was the kind of person I held up as the ideal: like she's this awesome Christian, this very bubbly, outgoing, sweet person, and nothing like this could ever happen to her—but it did, and if it could happen to her, it could to anybody. That by itself really helped me.

My depression didn't stop, but it did sort of fizzle. It took me a year to completely get out of it. I didn't take medicine or see counselors or anything (which, looking back, I probably should have).

But I got better—and then I went into medical school. That was a whole new kind of stress. I also had a whole lot of family issues, and I decided then that it was time to work on them. I come from a family where we don't talk about our problems in public. We don't talk about them to each other. For me to talk to a counselor who was a stranger ... yeah, I was not so thrilled about that.

My roommate was in school to be a family and marriage thera-pist, and she recommended me to a counselor she had shadowed. I went to see this counselor every two weeks for about a year. I never told my family. The counselor had helped me to understand why I felt the way I did, and she helped to understand my mood, my behavior, the way I react to other people, and to learn about boundaries.

The most recent season of depression was after I finished resi-dency (and I was probably depressed during my residency, too, just from the sheer fatigue of it all). I'm in this job where I'm not sure if it's where I'm supposed to be. I had that same feeling as the depression in college, where I was angry all the time, and I had to give myself a pep talk before I went into every patient room, because I was so anxious going in. I just didn't want to talk to anybody, and I was snapping at sweet little old ladies, and at my staff, who are awesome, and there was no reason to snap at them. I wasn't sleeping well and I was eating everything in sight. So I called one of my attendings, who was doubling in family medicine and psych. I asked for an appointment, and he said, "Sure—I've seen pretty much our whole staff."

I told him, "I'm not sure if I'm depressed or burned out." I hadn't had a vacation in nine months, and this could just be burnout. I talked to him for about an hour, and he concluded: "I think you're depressed *and* burned out. Here's your Prozac. Come back to see me in a month."

I ended up taking the maximum doses of two different medications, to get me back to feeling like a normal functioning member of society again. That's where I'm at now, and I just saw him for that follow-up. That month has made a difference. I'm not totally *back,* but I'm nice again in clinic. I'm more organized.

About that: Everyone's depression is different. For me, it's not so much about sadness, but irritability and the inability to focus. I can't keep a straight train of thought. I can't remember anyone's names. I'm usually the kind of doctor, who after seeing you once or twice, I know your entire medical history and all your prescriptions. But when I'm depressed, I just can't remember. In my residency, I thought it was because I was new and in a new environment, but having taken medicine, I figured out: it was the depression.

J: I know that wasn't easy to share. I wanted to pick up on several threads you mentioned, especially about how everyone's depression looks different. You experienced anger and irritability, and I think a lot of people who deal with anger don't know that it's actually a part of depression. It's easy to see "angry people" as dealing with narcissism or anger

management problems, which could possibly overlap, but I think anger as part of depression is such a covert, hidden thing.

For me, I also get angry when I'm depressed, and I get confused, because I wonder, "Am I angry because I'm a jerk and can't have self-control and discipline? Or is there a depression underneath?" Can you say more about that?

Dr W: If you want to use psych language, it's an *atypical depression*. The textbook definition of depression is usually about someone who is sad all the time, who can't sleep and only wants to eat, who are sluggish, and their mind is fuzzy. Atypical depression is not so much that you're sad (which did happen to me), but that every little thing people did irritated me. Patients calling for refills or calling me because they're still sick three days later ... just normal human behavior, which shouldn't irritate me, drove me nuts. My patience was non-existent. I'd complain to the nurses and they'd nod and smile and finally say, "Yeah, that's normal."

It got to the point where I wasn't enjoying my work. If I'm angry at little old ladies because they talk a lot or because they whine—well that's what little old ladies do. I realized, "This isn't me. *I'm not an angry person.*" I knew there had to be more to it than just anger.

J: The other thing here, in relation to atypical depression, is that many see depression as completely debilitating—but you were still going to the office, still working and functioning. I've heard this phrase "high-functioning depressive," where it's not, "The wind's knocked out of me and I can't get out of bed," but, "I'm at work and I just want to flip tables."

Dr W: Well ... I can't really say I was high-functioning, though. I mean I was working eighty hours a week, but I was always behind on my work. Each weekend I'd have one-hundred fifteen new patients to go over, and normally it takes me five minutes per patient, but in my depression it took me about forty-five minutes to get through one. I had written notes on them but I couldn't *get the words out*, I couldn't put my thoughts together well enough to get it on paper.

I was pushing through, but my office staff, they knew I was burning out. They told me, "You need a vacation. You're too tired and you're not getting stuff done."

So even though I was working, I was very inefficient. In the last month, it has improved dramatically, the amount of work I can do in the same amount of time.

J: I'm tempted to move on to the next question, but you were so vulnerable just now, and I really want to pause and slow down and sit with this. I can't imagine how overwhelming this was for you. You said you were working eighty hours per week, and it sounds like you were running through an iron blanket to get your work done.

Dr. W: I went to work at eight a.m. and stayed until eight at night, then spent all day Saturday and Sunday dictating notes, skipping church so that I could finish. I had one-hundred fifteen encounter notes that I had scribbled during appointments, but come the weekend, I couldn't make heads or tails of them.

J: Wow. I'm imagining the hundreds of thousands of people who must be living this way. That's staggering to me. Another thing you said that really jumped out is that you were praying for a *safe name*. For someone to talk to about what was happening. Do you think that's a necessary part of fighting depression?

Dr. W: Yes. I think talking about it is a huge part of it, especially for someone like me who came from a family who didn't talk about it. Maybe if you're from a family who's all emotions all the time, it's different—but for someone like me, who's used to bottling things up and dealing with them on my own, having someone to share that burden is necessary. I tell my patients, who can't always have access to a therapist, "Talk to your friend at church, talk to your neighbor, talk to your cousin, somebody that you trust, someone who can take some of the load off your shoulders."

Now not everyone is a safe person to talk to. Some people are going to judge you. Some people will say, "Why do you feel depressed? Just cheer up."

J: Well, I've never heard that one before. Hah.

Dr. W: Yeah, "I'll just stop being sick. I'll stop being diabetic and overweight." You have to find a person who might not even have any advice to offer, but who can listen. My friend didn't have much advice to offer me. She pretty much said, "I've been through that, too, and it really sucks."

J: Did you feel embarrassed or worried when you thought about reaching out to even a safe name?

Dr. W: Absolutely. Even now, after I've been through counseling, it took me a month to tell my friend recently that I needed to meet up. For one, getting the motivation ... I'd pick up the phone and the motivation went right out the window. But for two, telling someone, "I need help," is really embarrassing. When I did reach out and said I was depressed, my friend said, "Yeah—I think that's been obvious." She already knew.

J: So let's change gears with a new question. *Is depression a choice or a disease? And how is that important in fighting depression?*

Dr. W: I think, to some extent, it's both. It's probably more disease. At least in my case, I was depressed for no reason. There was no traumatic event that triggered it, though that's happened to me too, but illnesses can just happen.

I think there's also choice involved in how you deal with it. I hate to do that cliché of comparing it to diabetes, but diabetes is a disease and how you deal with it is a choice. How you take care of yourself makes a huge difference in your disease.

With depression, like any disease, if you ignore it, it gets worse, and if you deal with it head-on, it can get better. If you dwell on it, it can get worse. Especially on Tumblr, you see fourteen and fifteen year olds who have these terribly sad blogs with quotes from Sylvia Plath—if that's all you're dwelling on, then things won't get better. I mean, sometimes you just need to go pet a kitten. (I'm a cat person.) I got a Tumblr, so I know, it's easy to stay moping in your pity party. I've had to stop myself and just *go outside* and get sunshine.

There was a study a couple years ago about microbes that come up when you're digging in the dirt which help with depression.[117] I thought, "Well, yeah." I don't know how the science behind it works, but getting dirty and sweaty will help. The sun will help. Digging helps you feel more ... *grounded.*

J: I love puns—and that was a good one.

Dr. W: Hah. I mean I've laid in bed all day watching Netflix, which is fine, but there has to be a choice to do something better for yourself, whether it's getting medicine or getting therapy or talking to someone. I had to *snap out of it.*

J: The phrase you used, *snap out of it,* has been anathema in the community of mental illness. And I know we can't "snap out of" a disease. But you also said that we can *choose* how we treat the disease. Am I following you correctly?

Dr. W: Yes. The way I tried to treat it before was to try to "snap out of it," which didn't work. So I'm certainly not saying you can just tell yourself to get better, but I think you *can* choose where you focus your energy and attention.

J: I received an email from a Nigerian who found that depression had to be a "white man's sickness." How do you respond to this and is there a way to discern *real depression?*

Dr. W: I've been thinking a lot about this one. Let me start off with the caveat that I'm white, but I've traveled to enough coun-

---

[117] Christopher Lowry, et al., "Identification of an immune-responsive mesolimbocortical serotonergic system: Potential role in regulation of emotional behavior," *Neuroscience*, May 11, 2007, 146(2-5): 756–772.

tries to know that depression crosses many cultures. Some don't call it depression; they might call it "soul sickness" or a demon or just sadness. But even in my own patient population, it's certainly not just white people who get depressed, and the way it's experienced in each culture is different, too. Different individuals show their emotions differently. I know we both took Cultural Competency (in my med classes, in your chaplaincy education), and we learned that an Asian man might be stoic and a Hispanic woman might be emotive, but the latter isn't necessarily feeling "more" than the former.

There's also a different stigma in developing countries. Those in poverty might be dealing with depression, but there's the thought, "So is everyone else." And if everybody feels depressed, then "nobody's depressed," so nobody wants to tell each other how they actually feel.

There's a huge need for mental health resources in refugee populations and poverty-stricken areas because they don't even recognize they're depressed. It's all they've ever known. Maybe white people recognize it because they've had so many privileges.

J: To be fair, the person who wrote me the email from Nigeria does say he wrestles with depression. But I guess if he admitted it to people around him, he'd get the reply, "Yeah, our life is already hard here."

Dr. W: On top of that, in under-developed places, those with mental illness who are "taken care of by the government" have been placed in these awful institutions. To admit you have depression is asking to be locked up.

A doctor I know who's from Afghanistan has a brother who dealt with a severe depression, and his brother ended up in an institution there. They chained him to a pole. It seems like admitting depression in certain places is a worse alternative than dealing with it on your own.

J: That's awful. I definitely feel that growing up here in America, even in a Korean culture that didn't know what to do with mental illness, I was overly privileged to have safe names and places that I can go to.

I want to go back really quickly to the issue around Tumblr bloggers, who I know we both love, and I don't want to diminish them at all—but I've seen a fashionable "pseudo-depression" subculture on social media. Depression is sometimes used as a blog persona or calling card. There was one survey I got where the respondent said her friends used to compare scars from cutting. I don't think that's the norm, and maybe they really are depressed, which overlaps with their need for attention. But have you seen this? Do you know how we can approach it or confront it?

Dr. W: I've seen it, *a lot*. Some of it's attention-seeking, and I hate to say this in a judgmental way, but it's like the kid who acts out and gets punished—the bad attention is just as good as the good attention. I think it's for an ego boost, and people look for that wherever they can, even if that means posting pictures of cutting. All that may have started off as depression, but it eventually just feels good to get comments online saying, "I hope you feel better" over and over.

J: I want to throw in, just to be fair, that self-harm is due to a variety of factors. I don't know if it's all for attention. I want to believe that those who have to pretend they're depressed are really suffering, too. I'm sure there's an underlying issue of why the bandwagoning happens. I think we can dig deeper to find out.

Dr. W: I agree that the bandwagoning has to stop. I also agree there has to be some underlying reason, whether it's low self-worth, or you know, they're actually depressed.

J: Here's my next question. Do you have any particular stories about victories or defeats with depression?

Dr. W: I have a story about a defeat. I had a family friend, a good friend of my mother's, who was my boss for several years. She had bipolar disorder, and she was depressed almost all the time. She had been in and out of the hospital and never seemed to get better. When she wasn't depressed, she was super-fun and hilarious. But then she'd get unstable and spend thousands of dollars she didn't have.

She would make a suicide attempt, and she'd get better, and then she'd try to attempt suicide again. Soon she couldn't work anymore and lost her business and went bankrupt. She started going to therapy and taking meds and she was working again. She got better. Around that time, on the up-swing, there was a meeting and she didn't show up. Someone went to her house, and they found her on the kitchen floor covered in blood. She had slit her wrists. They got her to the hospital, got her all fixed up, and she got better.

But I didn't know how to help her anymore. I talked with my mom, who wanted to help her. I said plainly, "She has a disease, and you can try everything, but sometimes it wins."

Finally, my mother's friend shot herself. That was it.

At the funeral, the pastor carefully, wisely said, "She had a disease, and sometimes you don't get better until you get to Heaven." I sort of liked the way the pastor said that. He took the burden off her and it was not her fault.

That's the thing about disease. You can do everything to treat it, and you should, but sometimes it won't get better. But as a Christian, I do have hope that you get better on the other side. I believe she's there now. I guess that's a victory *and* a defeat. I don't really know how to put it ... It's not exactly either one, but she really is better now.

J: That's one of those times where there's no silver lining or a neat little bow tie at the end. I think at the same time, that her story validates that depression is a real monster, and it destroys people, and we as a community need to take that more seriously. I mean, it's heavy to think that one day my depression could win. It could have a terminal result. It's dark to say that, and I pray it won't happen—but I wish we took it that seriously, as serious as cancer.

Dr. W: Yes, a lot of times you hear about people "battling cancer," but no one thinks of battling depression. They think, "Oh, she's just dramatic."

And like fighting cancer, not everyone succeeds at fighting depression. I'm so glad that the pastor at the funeral didn't make it about "having enough faith" or saying "depression is a sin." Look at Elijah, who was suicidal, and no one's going to say he didn't have faith.

J: Yes! Elijah is my favorite Old Testament character. Going back to the theological piece, when you said, "She's in Heaven now"—there's something about suicide where Christians immediately condemn someone like that to hell. To me, that's absolutely unfair, and I don't think it's true. I also get upset when Christians say, "If you really had faith, you wouldn't be depressed!"

Dr. W: You think even about Jesus praying to have the "cup" taken from him, which is a whole different level of grief and despair. No one can ever say that having faith would exclude us from being depressed.

J: So two last questions. What methods have you found helpful to fight depression? And what would you say to someone in their worst moment of depression, right then and there?

Dr. W: For the first question: Every single human being can benefit from counseling at some point in their lives. We all go through something that we need to talk to somebody about. We need someone who has better tools than we do to help us figure out how to deal with it. If my toilet's broken, I call a plumber. If my brain is broken, I probably need counseling.

People are so embarrassed to get counseling though. A lot of my patients won't see a counselor, so I'll counter, "Would you come talk with me every two weeks?" They say, "Oh, yeah!" And I say, "Well, okay, that's counseling." Some people think counseling is, "They tell you what's wrong with you and you have to do all this stuff," and I have to say, "No. They listen to you and ask you questions and try to give you insight on your issue."

Another thing is, if you need medication, take the medication. Christians: *prayer and Zoloft are not mutually exclusive.*

You also have to think through the source of depression. I trace through the entire bio-psycho-social model of depression, and whichever cause is more dominant, you need to attack it from that angle. It could also be all three, so then, go after all three.

To answer your second question: I've had patients in my office who *are* in the worst moment of their depression. I don't have a line or anything, since everyone's different, and I wouldn't say the same thing to a forty-five year old as I would a middle schooler. But most of them are resistant to the idea of getting help. They might come to me for help, but then they're afraid to take the medicine or they're afraid of going to the hospital. And I have to tell them, "If you could just let me carry you for a short time—you can be angry at me—but let us get you better."

I had a patient who was livid that I sent him to the hospital, but I told him, "You are *not* safe to go home. I cannot in good conscience let you go back home. I wouldn't sleep tonight. I'd be wondering all night if you're going to turn up dead on the kitchen floor. I'll come see you at the hospital, and you can be mad at me, *but you'll be mad and alive.*"

They know, in the end, that I care about them. It's why they talked to me in the first place. Showing that I care is the best thing I can do. I tell them I'm going to call them later that day, then in a week to see if they're getting better or worse.

J: I guess this is a trick question, about "what to say" to someone when they're depressed, since there are no magic one-liners. The impression I'm getting is that it's your presence that's most important.

Dr. W: That's right. I had this friend in college who had a manic episode, and had been an alcoholic, and she snapped and told me she needed a drink. I said, "No, you don't. You can't, because I have your keys." She demanded her keys back, but I told her she had to stay at my place until she got better. So she stayed at my apartment for two days. We had ice cream and chocolate. I then took her to her doctor. All of that is more important than anything I have to say.

J: I love the idea you said earlier: *You'll be mad but you'll be alive.* It's like you're fighting their inner gravity which their brain is tricking them into, or like pushing them out of traffic.

Dr. W: Part of the disease process is that your brain feels like it's trapped. Every option seems wrong or you find some way to believe it won't work. So I have to step in there to say, *"If you can just let me be there, whether you think something will work or not, and let me be a part of that process, we can eventually unhook that trap and see there really are ways out, that you just can't see now. You'll look back and realize there was a way through that you couldn't have seen before."*

Chapter 11
Elijah, by Bread and Water

I Have Had Enough

About three-thousand years ago, a man named Elijah fled across a desert, a contract on his head. He was one of the last of the *nabi*, God's chosen mouthpieces, in the kingdom of Israel.

Only hours before, Elijah had scored an incredible victory. On the blood-drenched peak of Mount Carmel, Elijah had faced off with nearly a thousand bloodthirsty prophets of Baal and Asherah, the twin gods of fertility. The throng of prophets had called to their gods from morning to evening, demanding fire to arise from the altar, slashing themselves with swords and spears, their blood flowing crimson across the creases of the summit as a multitude of villagers and travelers stood by.

The twin gods did not answer.

Elijah prayed, and indeed *Yahweh*, the Living God, answered. Fire came down across the altar of Elijah, and the prophets of Baal and Asherah bowed down to worship *Yahweh*. The witnesses around the summit, as was the custom, enclosed the false prophets and destroyed them.

King Ahab, the corrupt king of the nation, is stricken with terror at the loss of his false prophets, and tells this news to his wife, the devious Queen Jezebel. The queen orders a hit and sends a messenger to tell Elijah:

"May the gods deal with me, be it ever so severely, if by this time tomorrow I do not make your life like that of one of those prophets."

I have wondered why Queen Jezebel didn't simply use the messenger as the assassin. Yet I am certain this was part of Jezebel's design: she desired to strike fear in the very heart of Elijah before striking down his flesh.

It worked. Elijah fled, in terror.

I am certain, too, that any other day, Elijah may have brushed off the threat to his life. It would not have been his first. He had also won the largest battle of his life, in a show of power witnessed by the skeptical citizens of Israel, and he had wiped out his sworn enemies, the prophets who had been conducting the sacrifices of children. Even more, *Elijah had heard directly from God.* Elijah had called down fire, and it had been so.

Yet, I imagine his exhaustion. All day, facing off against the false prophets. His loneliness, as one of the last of the *nabi.* His burden, as a preacher and healer to the kingdom. His travels, on foot, from towns that would not receive him.

Elijah fled to the desert.

He spent the day there, swaying in the shimmering heat, before collapsing under a juniper tree. Such a cursed tree would provide no shade, no shelter.

Elijah prayed:

"I have had enough, Yahweh. Take my life. I am no better than my ancestors."

I've been there. Have you, too?

I cannot stand this any longer. Just end it, God. I'm all out.

Then Elijah fell asleep under that slender, spindly tree.

At once, a different messenger visited — this one, an angel. The angel touched Elijah and said, *Arise, and eat.*

Elijah found a cake of bread over hot coals and a jar of water.

I think this may be one of my favorite parts of the story. *Yahweh* sends an angel, not to lecture, not to prod, not to press, but to offer sustenance. The angel also touches Elijah somehow, perhaps a hand on his shoulder, a warmth across his sternum, a coolness across his forehead. The angel tended to all of Elijah's needs.

After he ate, *Elijah falls asleep again.*

I love this part, too. Nap, food, and sleep. Who has never done this before?

The angel arrived a second time, with a touch and more food. This time the angel said, *Arise and eat, for the journey is too much for you.*

Elijah ate, and he regained his strength to keep moving, towards the mighty Mount of Horeb.

There, at the mountain, *Yahweh* showed His power — first, by a fierce wind that sheared off the face of the cliffs, and then an earthquake that fractured the mantle, and then a fire that melted the rocks to pumice and obsidian.

But *Yahweh* did not show Himself in any of these displays. Instead, *Yahweh* was a gentle whisper, telling Elijah: *Find Elisha, your successor, and anoint him.*

Elijah, revived by his new mission, trekked back across the desert, leaving differently from the man he was before.

> *"I remember my affliction and my wandering, the bitterness and the gall. I well remember them, and my soul is downcast within me. Yet this I call to mind and therefore I have hope: Because of the Lord's great love we are not consumed, for his compassions never fail. They are new every morning; great is your faithfulness."*
>
> — Lamentations 3:19-23

By Bread and Water, I Rise

I have always considered Elijah my favorite character in the Hebrew Scriptures of the Bible.

He is, somehow, both a man of great faith and a man who was ready to take his own life. Like King David, like Peter, like Thomas, like Paul, Elijah was a contradictory blend of highs and lows, of confidence and self-condemnation, of certainty and self-doubt.

James, the half-brother of Jesus, writes a thousand years later about Elijah: *He was a man just like us.*

I only have to look to Elijah to know that the God of the universe, the very one who crafted me from atoms to axons to an aorta, is a God who empathizes with my broken brain.

I will never, ever believe that depression is a "sin." I don't believe God "gave me depression." I don't think God is "teaching me a lesson" through suffering. I believe we live in a fractured, fraying world where darkness sometimes enters into our sacred creation, and that the thread of my being has been unraveled by the dark. I don't believe that depression is "God's plan for my life"—but it's still a part of my story, and I have to believe it's part of a greater glory, a richer, fuller portrait of all that makes us human and alive.

And whether by bread or water or a touch from a friend, God is there, a current of the divine, walking me home through the desert, until I am finally home with Him.

There's, too, a Body of Bread and Living Water that has come for me. There's, in Jesus, sustenance, the friend, the healer, the Greater *Nabi*, the authority over winds and mountains, a coursing fire, a gentle whisper, the God who became *a man just like me,* and loved me enough to stay on that cursed tree.

God, somehow, by becoming *one of us* in flesh-embodying solidarity, gets my depression, more than I can dare to fathom.

To know this love, even just a whisper in the weariness, can be enough.

—

I've been told:

"If you really had faith, you wouldn't be so depressed!"

But no—it's actually my faith that was the very last rock at the bottom, that kept me going right on through depression.

It's not that when you have faith, your depression is gone, but when you're depressed, your faith can help you through.

A Reminder to You, Dear Friend

You are loved.

You might have heard that a million times, but it's no less true.

You do have a Creator. He is with you. He is bigger than your situation and closer than your deepest hurt. He's not mad. He is cheering for you and rooting for you this very second. He's okay about all the things before. He sent His Son for that very reason.

You can put down the blade. You can throw away the pills. You can quit replaying those regrets in your head. You can quit the inner-loop of self-condemnation. You can forget your ex. You can walk away from the porn. You can resolve your conflicts right now. You can sign up to volunteer at that shelter. You can thank your parents for everything. You can hug the person next to you. You can tell the waiter, "Jesus loves you." You can go back to church. You don't have to sit in the back. You don't have to prove your worth to the people you've let down. You don't have to live up to everyone else's vision for your life. You're finally, finally free.

You are loved. I am loved.

As much as I love you, dear friend, He loves you infinitely more.

Believe it. Walk in it. Walk with Him.

God is in the business of breathing life into hurting places.

This is what He does, even for the least likely like you and me.

Conclusion
The Truth Is

I did a photo shoot a few years ago with a ton of smiles and silly faces—but this picture was a bit closer to how I was really feeling. It was during one of the most miserable seasons of life, when depression had hit full force and I was contemplating The End every waking moment. I had gained over twenty lbs. from binging and I randomly fell asleep in my office and I kept letting go of the steering wheel, daring myself to crash.

No one knew what was happening; I tried to tell someone but he laughed it off: "Look at you, how could you be so stressed when you're so blessed?" So I kept up the smiles and silliness, all while my insides were wax dipped in acid, melted to the thinnest thread, stretched between bones across a chasm. I was Zeno's paradox, motionless in motion. I was begging God to kill me.

I wanted to give up: but no. God said no. He was stubborn, and so I was, too. I hustled. I fought the dark with everything, both fists swinging, screaming and laughing at the same time, crawling by my bare fingernails to the lip of the well I had been cast down into. Slowly, painfully, somehow, I made it through, mostly because I kept waking up and was astounded to find myself still breathing, and because I gained ground by inches. Colors returned; the fog lifted over time; I found people I could tell; I got a dog and I lost the weight and I survived. It's not as romantic as it sounds, and I don't know if the next one will win. But the last time, I did. He did. God didn't answer my prayer then, and it was the best "no" that I've ever gotten. I'm here, just barely. So is He, completely.

— J.S.

Appendix

Here's a list of different treatments for depression.

- **Eye Movement Desensitization and Reprocessing (EMDR):** An evidence based treatment method for PTSD, although emerging research shows it can be effective for depression. EMDR uses bilateral stimulation in the brain through alternating auditory sounds, tapping, or eye movements to reprocess difficult memories and the negative beliefs that are attached to them. [118]

- **Acupuncture:** Eastern therapy in which needles thinner than a hair are placed in "pressure points," used for pain management or relaxation. It's not for everyone, but I can attest it has helped me.

- **Ketamine:** A highly controversial new finding in which ketamine acts as an instant killer of depression. However, ketamine is a narcotic with intense side effects such as psychosis and hallucinations. It's also very unlikely that your physician would prescribe this to you (perhaps until further research).

- **Deep Brain Stimulation (DBR) with Electrodes:** Another controversial finding in which the placement of certain electrodes in your brain, particularly in a place called Broddman area 25, can decrease depression over time. This work is being

[118] Francine Shapirom "The Role of Eye Movement Desensitization and Reprocessing (EMDR) Therapy in Medicine: Addressing the Psychological and Physical Symptoms Stemming from Adverse Life Experiences," *The Permanente Journal*, Mar. 2014, 18(1): 71–77

done by Helen Mayberg and Andres Lozano, among others.

- Electroconvulsive Therapy (ECT): This is the scary "electro-shock" therapy you've seen in movies, but is actually nothing like it's portrayed. It's highly controlled under anesthesia and is successful for a range of mental illnesses. It's often a last resort, used for a depression that's chronic, high risk, and not responsive to other treatment options. ECT can also cause memory loss.

- Therapy Robots: Patients who were given "virtual therapists" were shown to have significant reduction in depression, and in some cases, were more honest with the robots than with human doctors.[119,120] One of the robot's names was "Woebot."

- Exercise: This is obvious, but regular exercise, especially within group settings, is nearly as effective as counseling and can even prevent depression. Fun fact: It's more effective in group settings, like dance, martial arts, basketball, tennis, or a local gym class. Another fun fact: It's more effective to exercise with people who don't share your illnesses.[121,122]

[119] Kathleen Kara Fitzpatrick, Alison Darcy, Molly Vierhile, "Delivering Cognitive Behavior Therapy to Young Adults With Symptoms of Depression and Anxiety Using a Fully Automated Conversational Agent (Woebot): A Randomized Controlled Trial," *Depression and Mood Disorders*, Vol. 4, No 2., Apr.-Jun. 2017

[120] Gale M. Lucasa, Jonathan Gratcha, Aisha Kingb, Louis-Philippe Morencya, "It's only a computer: Virtual humans increase willingness to disclose," *Computers in Human Behavior*, Vol. 37, Aug. 2014, pp. 94–100

[121] Felipe B. Schuch, Davy Vancampfort, Simon Rosenbaum, Justin Richards, Philip B. Ward, Nicola Veronese, Marco Solmi, Eduardo L. Cadore, Brendon Stubbs, "Exercise as a treatment for depression: A meta-analysis adjusting for publication bias," *Journal of Psychiatric Research*, Mar. 2016, 77, pp. 42-51

[122] George Mammen and Guy Faulkner, "Physical Activity and the Prevention of Depression: A Systematic Review of Prospective Studies," *American Journal of Preventive Medicine*, Nov. 2013, Vol. 45, Iss. 5, pp. 649-657

- Diet: This is also obvious, but an unhealthy diet will not help depression. Some studies also point to inflammation or certain gut bacteria that might affect mood, which can potentially be linked back to diet.

- Art, Music, and Relaxation Therapy: As discussed in Chapter 3, any sort of relaxation technique can be helpful in many cases.

- Getting a Pet: It's not easy taking care of a pet, but having any sort of additional responsibility can actually help with mental illness.[123] Consider the cost, however, and that pets are not novelty items. I adopted my dog Rosco from the Humane Society during an incredibly brutal depression, and I am almost certain that he saved my life.

- Deep Breathing: Breathing-based meditation, such as those used in yoga, are helpful for even those who were resistant to antidepressants.[124] I've practiced a breathing technique called *dan jeon,* an ancient Korean art.

For my theological and philosophical take on pain and suffering, please consider my book *Mad About God: No Silver Livings, No Christian Clichés, No Easy Answers for Pain & Suffering.*

---

[123] Atul Gawande, *Being Mortal,* (NY: Metropolitan Books, 2014) pp. 123-125
[124] Anup Sharma, Marna S. Barrett, Andrew J. Cucchiara, Nalaka S. Gooneratne, and Michael E. Thase," A Breathing-Based Meditation Intervention for Patients With Major Depressive Disorder Following Inadequate Response to Antidepressants: A Randomized Pilot Study," *The Journal of Clinical Psychiatry,* Jan. 2017, 78(1):e59-e63

Method of Conducting Surveys

Throughout this book, I mention "surveys" that were taken online. These were informal, message-based surveys conducted through Facebook, Tumblr, Wordpress, and email, at various times, which began on May 18th, 2016.

I received nearly two hundred responses, totaling about 40,000 words. Some of the respondents did not answer all the questions. The respondents, upon my estimation, skewed about 65% female and 35% male, with about two-thirds Christian or religious, as young as high school and up to seventies. About a quarter of the respondents had taken or were taking medication for depression.

I asked the following questions:

1) Which parts of the conversation around depression really bother you?

2) What kind of dialogue have you found helpful?

3) Do you feel that depression is more of a disease or a choice? Why?

4) Has prescribed medicine been helpful? Why or why not?

5) How do you help a friend who's going through depression?

6) What does depression feel like?

Hotlines
(By no means a comprehensive list.)

- Suicide Hotline: 1-800-SUICIDE (784-2433)

- For the hearing impaired, contact the Lifeline by TTY at: 1-800-799-4889

- National Suicide Prevention Helpline: 1-800-273-TALK (8245)

- National Adolescent Suicide Helpline: 1-800-621-4000

- Postpartum Depression: 1-800-PPD-MOMS (773-6667)

Depression and Bipolar Support Alliance (DBSA): 1-800-826-3632

- Veteran's Crisis Line: 1-877-VET-2-VET (838-2838)

- Survivors of Bereavement by Suicide: (UK) 0844-561-6855

- beyondblue info line: (Australia) 1300-22-4636

- 24/7 Crisis Line: (Canada) 905-522-1477

- Lifeline Australia: 13-11-14

- Teléfono de la Esperanza: 902 500 002 (Barcelona), 91 459 00 50 (Madrid)

- Seoul, South Korea Hotline: (2) 715 8600, (2) 716 8600 (2) 717 8600, (2) 718 8600

Acknowledgements

Thank you to the nearly two hundred respondents who answered the surveys with such daring honesty. I have done my best to honor the spirit of your stories.

Thank you to the many, many test-readers who helped to catch not only grammatical errors and structural issues, but kept me on my toes about fact-checking, fairness, and further education and research. I incorporated many of your suggestions and I'm indebted to the dialogue we shared. Thank you to licensed therapist Amanda Jones and to Dr. W. for your medical expertise and insightful conversations. Thank you to Clarice Chan, Jen Smith, Abby Mansoor, Christine Goodnough, and so many more for your very thorough test-reading.

This book would not be possible without the presence and encouragement of my lovely wife. She watched as I wrote this book for over a year, piece by agonizing piece, after work shifts long into the night, researching madly over the dinner table. She listened as I read the book out loud to her. She sacrificed many of our days off while I continued to write, believing that this book might save even *one* life, which will have been worth it. She was with me as I endured sudden health problems over the winter, a car accident that totaled our car, a dragged-out identity theft, and as my father went to the hospital with a life-threatening illness: all incidents that nearly did me in. The day that I finished the book, I fell on the floor in our living room and cried and cried, and my wife was there, holding me.

Thank you to Andre, Austin, Pastor Paul, Ted, Jacob, Tim, Alex, and Samuel. Even if some of us don't talk like we used to, each of you have been alongside me through some major seasons of depression, and consequently, you have saved my life.

Made in the USA
Lexington, KY
07 November 2018